Blood Group Systems: Kell

Blood Group Systems: Kell

Editors

Barbara Laird-Fryer, MT(ASCP)SBB
Assistant Technical Director,
The Blood Center at Wadley
Dallas, Texas

Judith Levitt, MT(ASCP)SBB
Chief Technologist, Transfusion Services,
Parkland Memorial Hospital
Dallas, Texas

Geoff Daniels, PhD
Scientist, Medical Research Council
Blood Group Unit, Wolfson House
London, England

American Association of Blood Banks
Arlington, Virginia
1990

American Association of Blood Banks
1117 North 19th Street, Suite 600
Arlington, Virginia 22209

ISBN NO. 0-915355-80-9
First Printing
Printed in the United States

Library of Congress Cataloging-in-Publication Data

Blood group systems: Kell/editors, Barbara Laird-Fryer, Geoff Daniels,
Judith Levitt.
p. cm.
Papers presented at a seminar held Nov. 10-11, 1990 in Los Angeles.
Includes bibliographical references.
Includes index.
ISBN 0-915355-80-9
1. Blood groups—Kell system—Congresses. I. Laird-Fryer, Barbara
II, Daniels, Geoff. III. Levitt, Judith S.
[DNLM: 1. Blood Groups—congresses. WH 420 B6554 1990]
QP98.B5433 1990
612.1'1825—dc20
DNLM/DLC
for Library of Congress
90-949
CIP

Technical/Scientific Workshops Committee

Dennis M. Smith, Jr., MD, Chairman

Michael L. Baldwin, MBA, MT(ASCP)SBB
Alice Reynolds Barr, SBB(ASCP)
Daniel B. Brubaker, DO
Katherine B. Carlson, MT(ASCP)SBB
Morris R. Dixon, MM, MT(ASCP)SBB
Ronnie J. Garner, MD
Frances L. Gibbs, MS, MT(ASCP)SBB
Avrum H. Golub, MD
Christina A. Kasprisin, MS, RN
Sanford R. Kurtz, MD
Barbara Laird-Fryer, MT(ASCP)SBB
Judith S. Levitt, MT(ASCP)SBB
Leo J. McCarthy, MD
JoAnn M. Moulds, MS, MT(ASCP)SBB
Ronald A. Sacher, MD
Stephanie Summers, PhD, MT(ASCP)SBB
Phyllis Unger, MT(ASCP)SBB
Margaret E. Wallace, MHS, MT(ASCP)SBB
Robert G. Westphal, MD
Susan M. Wilson, MT(ASCP)SBB

Contents

Foreword

In 1986, the AABB Committee on Technical/Scientific Workshops began a series of programs and books on the blood group systems. This volume on the Kell system is the fifth in that series.

In this volume, the authors and editors have introduced the use of the nomenclature defined by the International Society of Blood Transfusion (ISBT) Working Party on Terminology for Red Cell Surface Antigens. The nomenclature established by this group was designed to be both eye- and machine-readable and to be in keeping with the genetic basis of blood groups. The introduction to the Kell system terminology is described in Chapter 1. The original terminology is often referred to parenthetically to assist the reader.

In the four decades since its discovery, Kell has developed from a single red blood cell antigen to a complex blood group system comprising at least 21 antigens. This book is devoted to the historical and recent developments in Kell system genetics, biochemistry, serology and association with disease. The clinical significance of various Kell system antibodies is addressed along with specific techniques that will aid in resolution of Kell system problems. The McLeod phenotypes and chronic granulomatous disease (CGD) are discussed at the genetical and biochemical levels, as well as in a chapter devoted to the phenotype and its relationship to several diseases.

The complexity of this system prevents this single book from relating every detail of the Kell system, but the authors have highlighted the most important aspects of the system. Their chapters and accumulated references should enable the reader to research the details of the vast publications by serologists, geneticists, biochemists and others.

Barbara Laird-Fryer, MT(ASCP)SBB
Judith Levitt, MT(ASCP)SBB
Geoff Daniels, PhD
Editors

In: Laird-Fryer B, Daniels G and Levitt J, eds.
Blood Group Systems: Kell
Arlington, VA: American Association
of Blood Banks, 1990

1

The Kell Blood Group System: Genetics

Geoff Daniels, PhD

I N THE FOUR DECADES since its discovery in 1946, Kell has developed from a single red blood cell antigen into a complex blood group system comprising at least 21 antigens. These antigens appear to be encoded by genes at a number of sub-loci of the *KEL* complex locus. There is also a null phenotype in which none of the Kell antigens is present on the red blood cells. Expression of Kell system genes may be modified by epistatic effects, both from genes within the *KEL* complex locus and from at least two regulator genes, one of which is X-borne. Surprisingly, the location of the *KEL* gene in the human genome is still to be mapped.

The prime purpose of this chapter is to describe the genetics of Kell antigens: in particular, the inheritance of individual antigens and their "allelic" relationship with certain other Kell antigens and the effects of epistasis on inheritance of Kell system antigens as a whole. Genetic linkage and gene mapping will also be discussed. In order for the genetics of a blood group system to be intelligible, the serology, frequency and distribution of the antigens must be understood. These topics and some of the history of the Kell system are also covered in this chapter. Kell serology is discussed in greater detail in Chapter 2 and Kell biochemistry is described in Chapter 3.

Some antigens, generally considered to be Kell system antigens, have not been shown to be controlled by genes at the *KEL* locus. These antigens are often referred to as the para-Kell antigens. This distinction may be considered trivial as there is

Geoff Daniels, PhD, Scientist, Medical Research Council Blood Group Unit, Wolfson House, London, England

now substantial evidence in favor of the para-Kell antigens being true Kell antigens. However, while this evidence remains inconclusive, the para-Kell antigens will be described separately from the Kell antigens in this chapter. In instances where Kell antigens are referred to collectively, this reference will generally include the para-Kell antigens.

Notation

Before any description of a complex blood group system it is important that the notation used to designate antigens, phenotypes, genes and genotypes be defined. Some of the original names for Kell antigens—K, k, Kp^a, Kp^b, Kp^c, Js^a, Js^b—are useful in that they indicate which of the antigens are antithetical (the products of alleles). However, this terminology gives no indication that these antigens belong to the same blood group system and it may be misleading. For example, the notation K and k suggests that *k* is recessive to *K* when, in fact, they are codominant. There are other anomalies: the antigen antithetical to Wk^a has been reported as Côté or K11, but never Wk^b.

The International Society of Blood Transfusion (ISBT) Working Party on Terminology for Red Cell Surface Antigens has devised a numerical notation for blood group systems and antigens.[1] It is based on the nomenclature originally proposed by Allen and Rosenfield[2] for the first five Kell antigens. The numerical notation for the Kell system, system 006, is shown in Table 1-1. Included are 21 antigens numbering from KEL1 (or 006001) to KEL24 (006024) with three previously numbered antigens, KEL8, KEL9 and KEL15, now obsolete. In line with the ISBT Working Party recommendations, the notation used in this chapter for Kell antigens, phenotypes, genes and genotypes will be as shown in Table 1-2, although the original notations will often be provided as well.

Kell Antigens and Their Inheritance

KEL1 and KEL2 (K and k)

In 1946, in the first report of the application of the direct antiglobulin test to detect sensitization of neonatal red blood cells with maternal Rh antibodies, Coombs, Mourant and Race[3] described an antibody of new specificity. This antibody, originally called anti-Kell and subsequently anti-K or anti-KEL1,

Table 1-1. Antigens of the Kell Blood Group System

Number	Name	Relative Incidence	Comments	References
KEL1	K	Low	Antithetical to KEL2	3, 4
KEL2	k	High	Antithetical to KEL1	5
KEL3	Kp^a	Low	Antithetical to KEL4 and KEL21	6
KEL4	Kp^b	High	Antithetical to KEL3 and KEL21	6, 7
KEL5	Ku	High	Only absent from K_0 cells	8
KEL6	Js^a	Low	Antithetical to KEL7	9-11
KEL7	Js^b	High	Antithetical to KEL6	11-13
KEL10	$U1^a$	Low		14, 15
KEL11	Côté	High	Antithetical to KEL17	16, 17
KEL12	Boc	High	Para-Kell	18-20
KEL13	K13	High	Para-Kell	21
KEL14	San	High	Para-Kell, may be antithetical to KEL24	22-24
KEL16	"k-like"	High	k-like but absent from McLeod cells	25
KEL17	Wk^a	Low	Antithetical to KEL11	17, 26
KEL18	K18	High	Para-Kell, not shown to be inherited	27
KEL19	Sub	High	Para-Kell	28
KEL20	Km	High	Only absent from K_0 and McLeod cells	25, 29, 30
KEL21	Kp^c	Low	Antithetical to KEL3 and KEL4	31, 32
KEL22	K22	High	Para-Kell	33
KEL23	K23	Low	Para-Kell, assigned biochemically	34
KEL24	C1s	Low	Para-Kell, may be antithetical to KEL14	35

KEL8 (Kw), KEL9 (KL) and KEL15 (Kx) are obsolete. KEL15 is now XK1.

reacted with the red blood cells of the husband and two children of the antibody producer and with about 7% of random blood samples.[4] Mendelian dominant inheritance of *K* was confirmed by Mourant (cited by Race and Sanger[36(p283)]) who showed that all of five individuals with K+ red blood cells had one parent with K+ red blood cells.

Table 1-2. Examples of Kell System Notations

	Original	Numerical
Antigens	K, k, Kp^a, Kp^b	KEL1, KEL2, KEL3, KEL4
Phenotype	K–k+ Kp(a–b+)	KEL:–1,2,–3,4
Genes	*K, k, Kp^a, Kp^b*	*KEL 1, KEL 2, KEL 3, KEL 4*
	K^0	*KEL 0*
Genotypes	kKp^b/kKp^b	KEL 2,4/2,4
	Ul^a/Ul	KEL 10/–10
	kKp^a/K^0	KEL 2,3/0

Three years later Levine et al[5] described anti-Cellano, an antibody antithetical to anti-Kell. As *k* had already been used[37] to represent the allele of *K*, the symbol k was subsequently adopted for the product of that gene.[5] The antigen k is now KEL2.

KEL 1 and *KEL 2* are codominant alleles. Numerous family studies have confirmed the allelic status of *KEL 1* and *KEL 2*.[36-39]

In tests on blood samples from nearly 10,000 predominantly Caucasian English blood donors cited by Race and Sanger,[36(pp284-5)] 9.02% were found to be KEL:1. From this figure the following gene and genotype frequencies can be calculated: *KEL 1*, 0.0462; *KEL 2*, 0.9538; *KEL 1/1*, 0.0021; *KEL 1/2*, 0.0881; *KEL 2/2*, 0.9097 (assuming *KEL 2* is the only allele of *KEL 1*). KEL1 is less common in Blacks and extremely rare in the Mongoloid people of eastern Asia and America[40] (Table 1-3). KEL1 achieves its highest level among people of the Arabian and Sinai peninsulas, where up to 25% may be KEL:1.

In addition to *KEL 2*, other alleles of *KEL 1* may exist. These are very rare and appear to be responsible for aberrant expression of KEL1. Kline et al[49] described a family whose red blood

Table 1-3. Incidence of Kell System Low-Incidence Antigens and Genes

Antigen	Population	Number Tested	% Positive	Gene Frequency	References
KEL1	English	9,875	9.02	0.0462	36
	Parisians	81,962	8.55	0.0437	41
	Finns	5,000	4.10	0.0207	14
	US Blacks	4,079	1.50	0.0075	11
	Japanese	14,541	0.02	0.0001	42
KEL3	Caucasians	18,934	2.28	0.0114	6, 36, 43, 44
KEL6	US Blacks	1,298	15.87	0.0828	10, 11, 45
	African Blacks	593	15.68	0.0818	46
KEL10	Finns	2,620	2.60	0.0131	14
	English	5,000	0	0.0000	14
	Swedes	501	0.20	0.0011	14
	Chinese	12	1 pos.		14
	Japanese	8,000	0.46	0.0023	47
KEL17	English	11,044	0.29	0.0058	26
KEL21	Japanese (Osaka)	4,442	0.32	0.0016	*
	Japanese (Miyagi)	5,974	0.18	0.0009	48

*Okubo Y, personal communication.

cells demonstrated weakened KEL1 expression in four genera-tions. KEL2, KEL4 and KEL7 antigens were expressed nor-mally. This inherited KEL1 variant appeared to be purely quantitative: adsorption of anti-KEL1 with red blood cells of the propositus removed all anti-KEL1 activity, although eight adsorptions were required compared with two adsorptions with KEL:1 control red blood cells. A possible qualitative KEL1 variant was described by McDowell et al,[50] who found a KEL1-like antibody in the serum of a woman whose red blood cells were KEL:1. Her red blood cells and those of her daughter expressed a weak KEL1 antigen that failed to react with her KEL1-like antibody, whereas the red blood cells of her son, like those of his father, appeared to have normal KEL1 antigen and did react with the mother's antibody.

KEL1 expression may be acquired.[51] During a terminal epi-sode of sepsis, a patient's red blood cells previously known to be KEL:-1,2 became KEL:1, as did KEL:-1 transfused cells. Postmortem blood samples contained a gram-positive organ-ism Streptococcus faecium. KEL:-1 red blood cells incubated with a culture containing disrupted S. faecium became KEL:1.

KEL3, KEL4 and KEL21 (Kp^a, Kp^b and Kp^c)

In 1957, Allen and Lewis[6] described anti-Kp^a (anti-KEL3) and anti-Kp^b (anti-KEL4), two antibodies believed to detect the prod-ucts of alleles. Kell became a complex blood group system in the following year when Kp^a (KEL3) and Kp^b (KEL4) were shown to be the products of alleles linked to KEL 1 and KEL 2 (Kk).[7] Family evidence confirmed this very close linkage: individuals who are phenotypically KEL:1,3 never receive both KEL 1 and KEL 3 from the same parent and never pass them on to the same child.[7,43,52,53] Despite numerous studies of families with propositi whose red blood cells were KEL:1,3, the KEL 1,3 gene complex is yet to be found: KEL 1 is always in cis with KEL 4 (KKp^b) and KEL 3 is always in cis with KEL 2 (kKp^a); the common gene complex is KEL 2,4 (kKp^b).

Tests with anti-KEL3 on just under 19,000 blood samples from predominantly Caucasian individuals from Europe and North America,[6,36,43,44] analyzed by Race and Sanger,[36(pp286-8)] showed 2.28% to be KEL:3; a gene frequency of 0.0114 for KEL 3 (Table 1-3). Only 1.21% of individuals with KEL:1 red blood cells are KEL:3.[36] Although about 9% of Caucasians have red blood cells that are KEL:1, only 2.7% of predominantly Caucasian Bosto-nians with KEL:3 red blood cells were KEL:1.[6] Very little is known about the frequency of KEL3 in other ethnic groups[40]; it has not been found in Blacks or in Japanese. KEL4 is a public antigen in all populations studied.

In 1979, Yamaguchi et al[31] found a Japanese blood donor with anti-KEL4 to have a previously unencountered Kell phenotype: KEL:−3,−4 with an otherwise unremarkable Kell phenotype. When tested with antibodies directed against low-incidence antigens, her red blood cells reacted with the serum containing anti-Levay.[32] Confirmation that her red blood cells were Levay-positive came from cross-adsorption studies using her red blood cells and those of the original person who was Levay-positive.[32] Levay, originally reported in 1945, was the first inherited private red blood cell antigen.[54,55] Study of the Japanese proposita's informative family proved that Levay is the product of an allele of *KEL 3* and *KEL 4* (that is, a third allele at the *Kp* sub-locus). Thus the persistence of 34 years' work was rewarded by finding this second Levay-positive sample and by Levay becoming a member of the Kell blood group system, a system its junior by one year. Levay was renamed Kp^c and numbered KEL21.

Several more people homozygous for *KEL 21* have been found in Japan following identification of anti-KEL4 in their serum[56] (Yamaguchi H, Okubo Y and Seno T, personal communication). Kikuchi et al[48] found another Japanese family with two KEL: −3,−4,21 members who appeared to be heterozygous for *KEL 21* and the Kell-null gene *KEL 0*. Other than the original Levay-positive proposita and her family, only one individual whose red blood cells are KEL:21 has been found outside Japan. This phenotypically KEL:3,−4,21 Spanish American with anti-KEL4 in his serum had a father and two children whose red blood cells were KEL:−3,4 (Lawson J and Gavin J, personal communication).

KEL6 and KEL7 (Js^a and Js^b)

Giblett in 1958[9] and Giblett and Chase[10] the following year, described a new antigen, Js^a (KEL6), present on the red blood cells of about 20% of Blacks in the Seattle area. None of 500 red blood cell samples from Caucasians was KEL:6. *KEL 6* segregated from most blood group systems but, because of the low incidence of KEL1 and KEL3 in Blacks, it was clear that it would be difficult to show independence from the Kell system.[9,10]

In 1963 Walker et al[12,13] found an antibody to a high-incidence antigen in the serum of a Black woman whose red blood cells and those of her four children were KEL:6. This antibody failed to react with the red blood cells of 13 of 1269

Black donors. Twelve of the 13 were tested with anti-KEL6 and all were positive. The antibody also failed to react with the red blood cells of two sisters. Because the red blood cells of their 10 children were KEL:6, it was concluded that the sisters were probably homozygous *KEL 6/6*. The antibody was therefore called anti-Js[b] (anti-KEL7).

The first hint that KEL6 and KEL7 might belong to the Kell system came from the observation by Stroup et al[11] that red blood cells of the Kell-null phenotype (K_0) were KEL:-6,-7. A search of 4000 Blacks revealed six propositi whose red blood cells were KEL:1,6 and the subsequent family studies suggested control of *KEL 6* and *KEL 7* by the *KEL* locus. This was confirmed by four large Brazilian families with propositi who were phenotypically KEL:1,6.[57]

KEL6 is almost completely confined to Africans and people of African origin.[40] The frequency of KEL:6 among American Blacks is about 16%, giving a frequency of 8% for the *KEL 6* gene (Table 1-3). KEL6 is very rare, although not unknown,[36(p288)] in Caucasians. It has not been found in Japanese.[58] Of 11,000 samples from American Blacks tested with anti-KEL7, 34 were KEL:-7.[59] The phenotype KEL:6,-7 has not been reported in a person of non-African origin.

KEL11 and KEL17 (Wk[a])

The original anti-KEL11 was found by Guévin et al,[16,60] in the serum of a French-Canadian woman (Mrs. Côté). It reacted with all red blood cells tested except for her own, those of two siblings and K_0 phenotype red blood cells, which lack all Kell system antigens. McLeod phenotype red blood cells, which show reduced expression of Kell antigens, did not react with Côté serum by the antiglobulin test, but did adsorb the antibody. Thus, Côté serum appeared to contain an antibody recognizing a new high-incidence antigen related to the Kell system.

Strange et al[26] noticed that an antibody to a low-incidence antigen, anti-Wk[a], reacted with 0.3% of samples from English blood donors but with only 0.1% of samples from donors whose red blood cells were KEL:1. None of 1000 KEL:3 donor samples was Wk(a+). Six months of screening with anti-KEL1 in two regional transfusion centers, and then testing of the KEL:1 samples with anti-Wk[a], revealed seven KEL:1 Wk(a+) donor samples. Studies of the families of five of these donors showed that *Wk[a]* was always inherited with *KEL 2*: there was no recombinant and 13 nonrecombinants. Thus, Wk[a] appeared to be a new low-incidence Kell antigen and numbered KEL17.

Gavin (cited in Strange et al[26]) found that two KEL:–11 samples were KEL:17. Subsequently, Sabo et al[17] showed that KEL:–11 red blood cells from three more unrelated individuals were KEL:17 and confirmed, by two family studies, the allelic status of *KEL 11* and *KEL 17*. So *KEL 11:17* appears to be a fourth sub-locus of the *KEL* gene.

KEL10 (Ul[a])

An antibody, found through an incompatible crossmatch and shown to react with the red blood cells of 2.6% of Helsinki blood donors, was named anti-Ul[a] by Furuhjelm et al[14] in 1968. Tests on 18 families with propositi whose red blood cells were Ul(a+) showed that Ul[a] did not belong to most of the established blood group systems but provided no information about independence from Kell.

Despite the relatively low incidence of KEL1 in Helsinki (4.1%), by the following year three families with members who were phenotypically KEL:1 Ul(a+) virtually proved that Ul[a] is another antigen belonging to the Kell system.[15] There was no recombinant and 13 nonrecombinants between *Ul* and *KEL 1:2* (*Kk*), giving a lod score of 3.3 at a recombination fraction of zero. In all three families *Ul[a]* was inherited with *KEL 2*.

The existence of KEL:1,2,10 and of KEL:3,4,10 red blood cell phenotypes, with normal expression of Kell antigens, shows that *KEL 10* is not an allele at the *KEL 1:2* (*Kk*) or *KEL 3:4:21* (*Kp*) sub-loci. The possibility that *KEL 10* is a third allele at either the *KEL 6:7* (*Js*) or *KEL 11:17* sub-loci has not been eliminated.

The theoretical anti-Ul[b], an antibody detecting the product of the allele of *KEL 10*, has not been found. In its absence, the relationship of KEL10 to other Kell antigens will be difficult to elucidate. None of the red blood cells lacking the high-incidence para-Kell antigens described below is KEL:10.

Although KEL10 is generally considered to be a predominantly Finnish characteristic, 0.46% of Japanese[47] and one of 12 Chinese[14] had KEL:10 red blood cells (Table 1-3).

The Kell-Null Phenotype, K₀, and KEL5 Antigen (Ku)

K₀ Phenotype

In the same year as the discovery of KEL3 and KEL4,[6] Chown et al[61] found a new Kell phenotype, KEL:–1,–2,–3,–4, in two sisters whose consanguineous parents and two other sisters were of the common Kell phenotype KEL:–1,2,–3,4. The proposita had made an antibody that reacted with all but KEL: –1,–2,–3,–4 red blood cells. This antibody was used to search for another example of the new phenotype.[62,63] The 3122nd blood tested did not react and was also KEL:–1,–2,–3,–4. The parents of this donor were first cousins and because of this parental consanguinity, it was assumed that homozygosity for a rare gene, named K^o by Allen et al[7] and called *KEL 0* here, was responsible for the KEL:–1,–2,–3,–4 or Ko phenotype.

Race and Sanger[36] compiled information on 14 families of propositi whose red blood cells were K_o. These gave a sibling count of nine K_o and 29 not K_o, a ratio of 1:3.22, very close to the 1:3 ratio expected for a recessive gene. In at least four of these families the parents of the propositus were cousins, further evidence that the K_o phenotype results from homozygosity of a rare recessive gene. This gene is inherited at the *KEL* complex locus and is not an unlinked inhibitor gene. In several families heterozygosity for a silent gene producing no KEL1 or KEL2 explains abnormal inheritance of these antigens. One such family was described by Nunn et al[64] in which a KEL:–1,2 man with a KEL:1,–2 wife had children whose red blood cells were KEL:–1,–2, KEL:1,–2 and KEL:–1,2. Their probable genotypes are shown in Fig 1-1. To date, only one genetical background appears to be responsible for K_o. It is likely that *KEL 0* represents a deletion of part or all of the *KEL* gene, although this will remain hypothetical until the gene has been analyzed at the molecular level.

K_o red blood cells completely lack expression of all Kell antigens and, by definition, the para-Kell antigens, KEL5 and KEL20. Kx antigen strength is enhanced (see below). K_o red blood cells demonstrate no morphological abnormalities[65] or unusual expression of antigens belonging to other blood group systems.

Chown et al[44] found one K_o sample from testing 16,518 random Caucasians with the serum of the original K_o proposita.[61] Results of several studies that would have revealed K_o provided only one K_o sample from 24,953 Caucasians (data compiled by Race and Sanger[36(p294)]). These results suggest an incidence of about 0.007 for the *KEL 0* gene in Caucasians. Hamilton and Nakahara[42] found one K_o sample among 14,541 Japanese, suggesting a similar gene frequency.

KEL5 (Ku)

KEL5, originally named Ku,[8] is present on all red blood cells apart from those of the K_o phenotype, although its expression

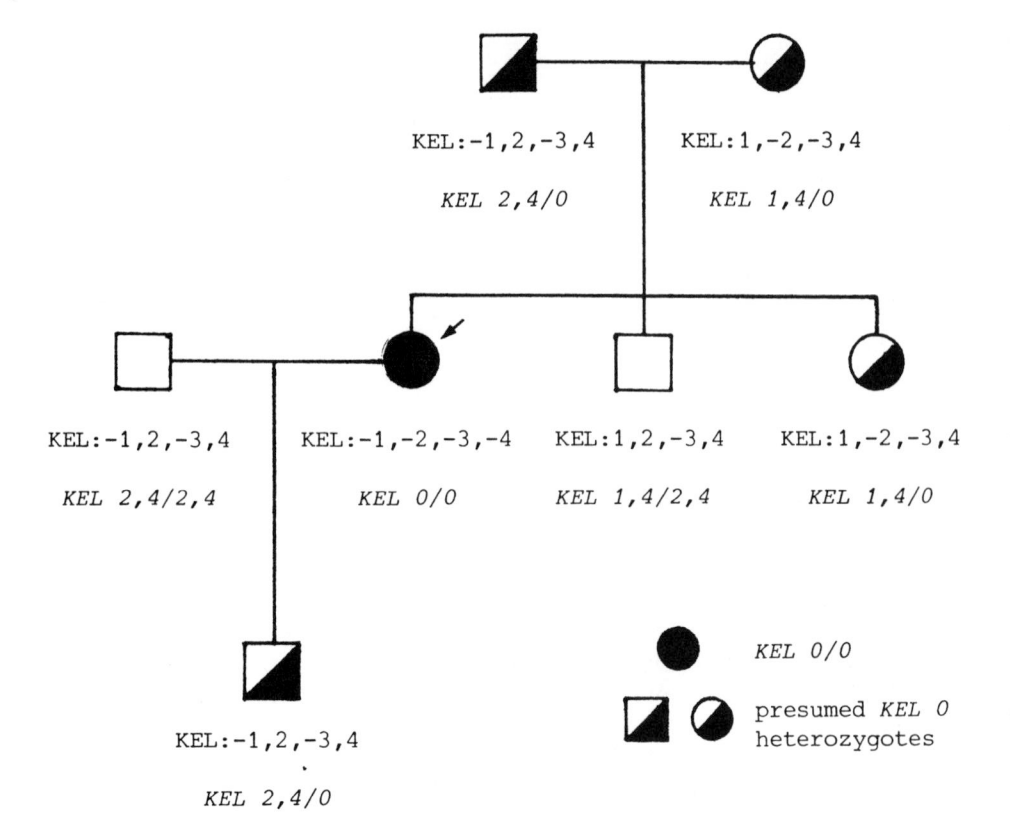

Figure 1-1. Part of family described by Nunn et al[64] showing Kell phenotypes and presumed genotypes and demonstrating unusual inheritance of KEL1 and KEL2 explained by the presence of a *KEL 0* gene.

may be modified in some other rare phenotypes (see below). Anti-KEL5 is the typical antibody of immunized individuals with the K_o phenotype. It appears to be a single specificity and cannot be separated, by adsorption and elution, into components of other Kell specificity.[8] Race and Sanger[36(p293)] list 10 examples of anti-KEL5 and many more have been found since. Two K_o individuals with anti-KEL4 and not anti-KEL5 have been reported[66] (Kuze M and Scott M, cited Race and Sanger[36]).

KEL Haplotypes

The genetics of the Kell antigens described above suggest that there are at least 4 sub-loci of the *KEL* gene—*KEL 1:2* (*Kk*), *KEL 3:4:21* (*Kp*), *KEL 6:7* (*Js*) and *KEL 11:17*. KEL10 and the para-Kell antigens (to be discussed below) suggest that several more *KEL* sub-loci may exist. Whether these all truly represent sub-loci at the *KEL* locus creating variations in the amino acid sequence at different positions on a single polypeptide chain, or whether they are separate, very closely linked, genes producing different proteins, cannot be demonstrated by conventional genetics. No family study has been reported revealing recombination as a consequence of crossing over within the *KEL* gene or showing more than one of the lower frequency characters to be inherited together, as part of the same complex or haplotype. Biochemical evidence that the high-incidence Kell system antigens are all carried on the same glycoprotein suggests that they are probably all encoded by the same gene[67] (Chapter 3). The known *KEL* haplotypes, assuming *KEL 10* to be at a separate sub-locus, are shown in Table 1-4.

Para-Kell Antigens

KEL12, KEL13, KEL14, KEL18, KEL19 and KEL22 are antigens of very high incidence dubbed para-Kell antigens by Race and Sanger.[36] They are absent from K_o red blood cells and expressed only weakly on McLeod phenotype red blood cells. Unlike KEL2, KEL4, KEL7 and KEL11, which share those characteristics, they have not formally been shown to be controlled by the *KEL* complex locus. Each of the antibodies detecting these antigens reacts with red blood cells lacking other high-incidence Kell or para-Kell antigens. All except KEL18 have been shown to be inherited and all except KEL18 have been shown to be located on the Kell glycoprotein.[67] This does not provide proof, however,

Table 1-4. The Eight Known Kell Haplotypes (in Two Notations) and Their Approximate Frequencies in Predominantly Caucasian English, US Black and Japanese Populations (Assuming *KEL 10* to be at a Separate Sub-locus)

Haplotype		Frequency		
		Caucasian	Black	Japanese
KEL 2,4,7,–10,11	$k\ Kp^b\ Js^b\ Ul\ K^{11}$	0.929	0.910	0.989
KEL 1,4,7,–10,11	$K\ Kp^b\ Js^b\ Ul\ K^{11}$	0.046	0.007	very rare
KEL 2,3,7,–10,11	$k\ Kp^a\ Js^b\ Ul\ K^{11}$	0.012	unknown	unknown
KEL 2,21,7,–10,11	$k\ Kp^c\ Js^b\ Ul\ K^{11}$	very rare	unknown	0.001
KEL 2,4,6,–10,11	$k\ Kp^b\ Js^a\ Ul\ K^{11}$	very rare	0.083	unknown
KEL 2,4,7,10,11	$k\ Kp^b\ Js^b\ Ul^a\ K^{11}$	very rare	unknown	0.002
KEL 2,4,7,–10,17	$k\ Kp^b\ Js^b\ Ul\ Wk^a$	0.006	unknown	unknown
KEL 0	K^0	0.007	very rare	0.008

that the para-Kell antigens are produced by the *KEL* gene. Marsh and Redman[68] point out that, despite Kell antigens being located on the same glycoprotein, the biochemical basis for intragroup specificity in the Kell system is still unknown and that immunodominant sugars provide one possible explanation. If expression of any of the Kell or para-Kell antigens were determined by oligosaccharides on the Kell glycoprotein, then the primary products of the genes controlling expression of these antigens would be glycosyltransferases and those genes would be at different loci.

Epistatic effects on the expression of *KEL* genes, both of the cis modifying type (see cis modifying genes) and unlinked suppressor type (see McLeod phenotype and Gerbich negatives), effect expression of the *KEL* and para-*KEL* genes in an identical way. This provides strong evidence in favor of para-Kell antigens being controlled by the *KEL* gene, but remains inconclusive while the true natures of the epistatic effects are unknown.

Two low-incidence antigens, KEL23 and KEL24, can conveniently be placed in the para-Kell category: the former for biochemical reasons and the latter because it is probably antithetical to one of the high-incidence para-Kell antigens.

KEL12

Four examples of anti-KEL12 and three propositi whose red blood cells were KEL:-12 have been reported.[18-20] All are Caucasian (although one was originally described as Black[69]). The third propositus had nine siblings, one whose red blood cells were also KEL:-12.[20] Their mother's red blood cells were KEL:12 and, although their father's red blood cells were not tested, consanguinity of the parents suggested that their KEL:-12 phenotype probably resulted from homozygosity for a rare recessive gene. Both KEL:-12 siblings suffered from gastrointestinal ulcers, both had been transfused and both had anti-KEL12.

KEL13

Marsh et al[21] described the first example of anti-KEL13 and the only reported propositus whose red blood cells were KEL:-13, a much transfused man of Italian parentage. The antibody in his serum failed to react with the red blood cells of one of his five siblings, a sister who had not made anti-KEL13 despite having seven children. The red blood cells of the propositus and his sister displayed weakened expression of KEL2, KEL4, KEL5, KEL7 and KEL12 antigens and, typical of red blood cells from a *KEL 0* heterozygote, gave an enhanced score with anti-Kx. It was proposed[21] that the KEL:–13 siblings are heterozygous for *KEL –13* and *KEL 0* and that the *KEL –13* gene has a suppressing effect on other Kell system genes in cis, a similar effect to that already known to occur in individuals with a *KEL 3* gene on one chromosome and a *KEL 0* gene on the other. The parents were not known to be consanguineous. It would be imprudent to draw genetical conclusions from dosage studies alone, but if this KEL:–13 phenotype were due to a *KEL –13/0* genotype, KEL13 would be considered a Kell rather than a para-Kell antigen.

The second example of anti-KEL13 was an autoantibody eluted from the KEL:13 red blood cells of a woman with autoimmune hemolytic anemia.[70]

KEL14 and KEL24

After an earlier brief mention,[18] the original anti-KEL14, found in the serum of a Caucasian woman, was described by Wallace et al[22] in 1976. KEL14 was shown to be an inherited character retrospectively when a previously described[23] public antigen, Dp, was shown to be KEL14.[24] The Caucasian proposita, whose red blood cells were KEL:–14, had six siblings: four who were phenotypically KEL:14 and two whose phenotype was KEL: –14.[23] The phenotype of her parents was KEL:14. They were first cousins.

An antibody in the serum of a Caucasian woman, which reacted with the red blood cells of her baby and the baby's sister, father, two paternal uncles and paternal grandfather, was numbered anti-KEL24.[35] *KEL 24* appeared to be the allele of *KEL 14*. The assumption that the antibody was detecting the product of an allele of *KEL 14* was derived from the following observations: anti-KEL24 reacted with all three KEL: –14 samples tested but with none of 700 other red blood cell samples and anti-KEL24 gave a higher titer with KEL:–14 red blood cells than with KEL:14,24 red blood cells. Anti-KEL24 did not react with KEL:24 red blood cells treated with 2-aminoethylisothiouronium bromide (AET).

KEL18

KEL18 is the only para-Kell antigen not yet shown to be inherited. Only one example of anti-KEL18 has been described and this antibody was made by a Caucasian woman, the only known person who has the KEL:–18 phenotype but does not have the K_o phenotype.[27] No further example of the KEL:–18 phenotype was revealed by tests on 54,450 blood donors.[71]

KEL19

The first anti-KEL19 was found by Sabo et al[28] in a woman whose red blood cells were KEL:–19. She had a brother of the KEL:–19 phenotype and two sisters of the KEL:19 phenotype. The second anti-KEL19, identified in the serum of a Black man, was used to test red blood cells of 10,757 donors: none was KEL:–19.[72]

KEL22

The first example of anti-KEL22, described by Bar Shany et al,[33] was found in the serum of an Israeli woman of Iranian Jewish origin. Her red blood cells and those of one of her three sisters were KEL:–22.

The family of the second KEL:–22 proposita, also an Iranian Jew living in Israel, provided some evidence of genetic linkage between *KEL 22* and *KEL 2*.[73] The family is shown in Fig 1-2. The parents (I-1 and I-2), whose red blood cells are KEL:22, are both *KEL 1/2*. They are first cousins. All three siblings (II-1, II-4 and II-5) whose red blood cells are KEL:–22 are *KEL 2/2* and the two siblings whose red blood cells are KEL:22 are KEL:1 (II-2 is *KEL 1/1* and II-3 is *KEL 1/2*). Therefore, in this family, *KEL 2* is traveling with *KEL –22* and *KEL 1* is traveling with *KEL 22*. This gives a lod score of 1.512 at a recombination fraction of zero, suggestive of close linkage but not statistically significant. The rule that no Kell system haplotype contains more than one lower incidence gene has not been violated by this family.

KEL23

KEL23 is a low-incidence antigen whose para-Kell status is based entirely on biochemical evidence. Marsh et al[34] found that the antibody of a Caucasian woman of Italian ancestry reacted with red blood cells of her two children, her husband and his mother but with none of 2100 reference samples. Biochemical investigations showed that the antigen, immuno-precipitated with the woman's antibody from her husband's red blood cells, resided on the 93,000 molecular weight Kell glycoprotein. The antigen was designated KEL23. Red blood cells lacking the high-incidence para-Kell antigens were all

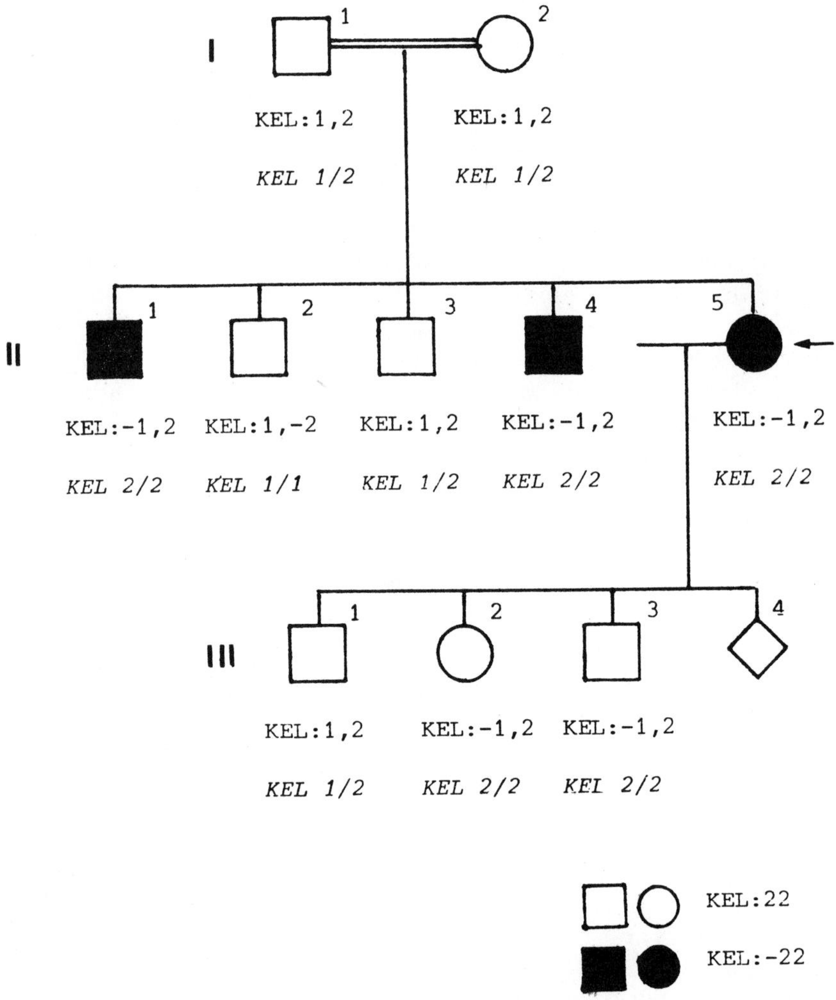

```
I          ⬜1 ══════ ⭕2
        KEL:1,2      KEL:1,2
        KEL 1/2      KEL 1/2

II   ⬛1      ⬜2      ⬜3      ⬛4      ⭕5  ←
      1        2        3        4        5

   KEL:-1,2  KEL:1,-2  KEL:1,2  KEL:-1,2    KEL:-1,2
   KEL 2/2   KEL 1/1   KEL 1/2  KEL 2/2     KEL 2/2

III      ⬜1      ⭕2      ⬜3      ◇4
          KEL:1,2    KEL:-1,2  KEL:-1,2
          KEL 1/2    KEL 2/2   KEL 2/2
```

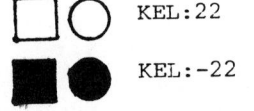

⬜⭕ KEL:22

⬛⬤ KEL:-22

Figure 1-2. Family described by Manny et al[73] showing inheritance of *KEL 22* with *KEL 1* and of *KEL –22* with *KEL 2*.

KEL:–23, showing that *KEL 23* is not the sole allele of any of the high-incidence para-Kell genes.

Depressed Kell Phenotypes

There are a number of rare phenotypes in which all or most of the high-incidence Kell and para-Kell antigens are expressed only weakly. The degree of depression varies. These depressed

Kell phenotypes arise from different genetic backgrounds and some appear to be acquired and possibly transient. The inherited depressed phenotypes will be considered first.

McLeod Phenotype, Kx Antigen and the XK Locus

McLeod Phenotype

McLeod, a rare blood group phenotype, is only one of a number of characteristics, including acanthocytosis and a variety of muscular and neurological defects, which collectively make up a wider phenomenon known as McLeod syndrome.[74] This syndrome is also sometimes associated with chronic granulomatous disease (CGD), an inherited disorder that impairs the functioning of phagocytes resulting in severe susceptibility to infection. McLeod syndrome will be described in detail in Chapter 4. In this chapter only the McLeod red blood cell phenotype, its inheritance and the probable reason for the association with CGD will be discussed.

Routine tests on medical students led Allen et al[75] in 1961 to recognize that one of the students, Mr. McLeod, had an unusual Kell phenotype. Initially it was thought that his red blood cells lacked all Kell system antigens and thus represented another example of the K_o phenotype. However, subsequent investigations revealed weak KEL2 and KEL4 antigens. KEL1, KEL3 and KEL5 antigens were not detected.

Since 1961 over 60 men and boys with McLeod phenotype have been identified.[68] Examples are described elsewhere.[25,29,65,76-89] All high-incidence Kell antigens are expressed on McLeod phenotype red blood cells but show weakened expression. The degree of depression of these antigens varies in different individuals with the McLeod phenotype. KEL1 is also weakly expressed when present.[85]

McLeod phenotype is very rare and no frequency estimates have been published. Swash et al[84] reported that two unrelated men with the McLeod phenotype were found as a result of testing, with anti-KEL2, red blood cells from many thousands of donors from South East England. With one exception,[82] all reported McLeod phenotype individuals have been Caucasian.[68]

Kx and KEL20 (Km)

The second example of the McLeod phenotype was recognized by van der Hart et al[29] in a 5-year-old boy afflicted with

recurrent infections, later presumed to be CGD. He had suffered a hemolytic transfusion reaction due to anti-KL, an
antibody that reacted with all red blood cells tested including
those of the K_o phenotype, except for his own and those of Mr.
McLeod. The term anti-KL actually represents two separable
antibodies.[25,29] One component, anti-Kx, can be separated from
the other by adsorption onto and elution from K_o red blood
cells. Anti-Kx reacts strongly with K_o red blood cells, weakly
with red blood cells of common Kell phenotype and not at all
with McLeod phenotype red blood cells[25] (Table 1-5). Adsorption of the "anti-KL" serum with K_o red blood cells removes
anti-Kx and isolates the other antibody, originally[25] also called
anti-KL but later[30] anti-Km or anti-KEL20. Anti-KEL20 reacts
with red blood cells of common Kell phenotype but not with K_o
or McLeod phenotype red blood cells[25] (Table 1-5).

Heterozygosity for the null gene at the *KEL* locus, *KEL 0*,
cannot generally be determined by titrations with antibodies
to high-incidence Kell antigens.[25,90] Anti-Kx is a tool for detecting red blood cells of *KEL 0* heterozygotes as it gives a titration
score intermediate between that for red blood cells from *KEL 0*
homozygotes and that for red blood cells from individuals with
no *KEL 0* gene.[25] Marsh et al[21] used anti-Kx for this purpose in
studying their propositus, whose red blood cells were KEL:–13,
and they suggested that his genotype was probably *KEL –13/0*
and not *KEL –13/–13* (homozygous for the rare gene that
produces no K13 antigen). Unfortunately, the procedure of
separating anti-Kx from anti-KEL20 is often difficult and sera
containing these antibodies are in very short supply.

Artificial K_o red blood cells, made by treatment of red blood
cells of common Kell phenotype with 2-aminoethylisothiouron-
ium bromide, like "natural" K_o red blood cells, have high
expression of Kx.[91]

Table 1-5. Expression of Kx, KEL20 (Km) and KEL5 (Ku) Antigens on Red Blood Cells of Common, K_0, McLeod and K_{mod} Phenotypes

Phenotype	Kx	KEL20	KEL5*
Common	weak	strong	strong
K_0	strong	negative	negative
McLeod	negative	negative	weak
K_{mod}	strong	**	weak

*KEL5 represents all high-incidence Kell antigens.
**not tested

The somewhat reciprocal relationship between expression of Kx and expression of Kell antigens suggests that Kx may be a precursor of Kell system antigens, this putative precursor being mostly used up in red blood cells with normal Kell expression but not in K_o red blood cells, which lack Kell system antigens.[25] There is no biochemical evidence, however, in support of this theory (see Chapter 3).

Anti-Kx plus anti-KEL20 appears to be the typical immune response of McLeod phenotype CGD patients following transfusion.[25,29,76] Yet, both of the only two non-CGD McLeod individuals reported to have been transfused made anti-KEL20 but no anti-Kx,[81,92] even though one was transfused with K_o red blood cells.[92] One autoanti-Kx in a man with common Kell phenotype has been reported.[93]

Inheritance of McLeod Phenotype and Kx Antigen

McLeod phenotype is inherited as an X-chromosome-linked recessive character: it has only been found in males and the rare gene is inherited from the mother not the father. Thus, expression of Kx antigen, present on all red blood cells save those of the McLeod phenotype, is controlled by an X-borne gene. The *KEL* locus is not X-borne and Kx cannot be considered a Kell antigen. Consequently, KEL15, at one time the numerical notation for Kx, is now obsolete.[1] The ISBT Working Party has awarded Kx system status with XK as the system symbol and 19 as the system number.[1] Kx is the only antigen within that system and has the ISBT number XK1 or 019001.

Chronic granulomatous disease may be either autosomal or X-linked.[94] Only a small minority of CGD patients have the McLeod phenotype: all have been of the X-linked type.

Marsh et al[65] proposed the symbol *Xk* for the gene locus controlling Kx expression. Four alleles at this locus were postulated to explain four phenotypes: X^1k, the comon allele responsible for normal Kx production; X^2k responsible for CGD associated with McLeod phenotype; X^3k responsible for X-linked CGD with normal Kell phenotype; X^4k, responsible for the McLeod phenotype, but no CGD. The symbol *Xk* has subsequently been changed to *XK*. It now appears that the locus for X-linked CGD and the *XK* locus are discrete and that McLeod phenotype associated with CGD probably results from a deletion of part of the X-chromosome, which includes both genes[86-89] (see below). Therefore, only two alleles at the *XK* locus should now be considered: *XK 1* (previously X^1k), which produces Kx (XK1) antigen, and *XK 0* (previously X^4k), which does not produce Kx and results in the McLeod phenotype (XK:–1).

Further evidence that the *KEL* genes do not contribute positively to the McLeod phenotype is provided by a family in which two brothers had the McLeod phenotype yet had different Kell phenotypes.[85] One brother's red blood cells were KEL:–1,w2 and the other's were KEL:w1,w2 (where w denotes weak expression of the antigen). Thus one had inherited *KEL 1* and the other *KEL 2* from their father, whose red blood cells were KEL:1,2 with normal expression of Kell antigens.

X-Chromosome Inactivation

Although the somatic cells of female mammals possess two X chromosomes, only one is active. Inactivation of one of the X chromosomes occurs at an early stage in embryological development when a few million cells have been formed. Whether the maternal or paternal X chromosome in any cell becomes inactive is generally a matter of chance but, once inactivation has taken place, all descendants of that cell will have the same inactivated X chromosome. So the female adult is a mosaic of clones of somatic cells, some with the maternal X chromosome active and the others with the paternal X chromosome active. Consequently, a woman heterozygous at an X-borne locus would be expected to express each allele in approximately half of her cells and no cell would express both alleles.[95] An exception to this rule concerns genes at the very tip of the short arm of the X chromosome, the region of pairing between X and Y chromosomes, which escape inactivation and include the *XG* blood group locus.[96]

If *XK* were subject to inactivation, red blood cells of mothers, daughters and half of the sisters of McLeod phenotype males would be expected to comprise two separate populations of McLeod and normal red blood cells. Marsh et al[97] demonstrated that the red blood cells of the mother of a McLeod phenotype CGD patient were indeed a mixture of Kx+ and Kx– red blood cells and mixed populations of red blood cells have since been recognized in many female carriers of *XK 0*, the gene responsible for the McLeod phenotype.[56,78,80-82,84,85,98] The proportion of McLeod phenotype red blood cells in female McLeod carriers varies from 5-85%.[68] This dual population of red blood cells is often difficult to detect serologically, especially if Kell antibodies and not anti-Kx are used. However, flow cytometry permits an accurate estimation of the two red blood cell types present.[68]

Location of XK on the X Chromosome

XK was assigned to the X chromosome through the characteristic mode of inheritance of Kx and the McLeod phenotype. *XK* and the *CGD* gene appear to be linked to *XG*,[99,100] although the position of these genes on the X chromosome makes this unlikely (Fig 1-3). Recombination between *XG* and *XK*[81,84] and between *XG* and the *CGD* gene[56] (Marsh, cited in Wolff et al[100]) has been recorded. Whereas *XG* is on the X-Y pairing region near the telomere of the short arm of the X chromosome and escapes inactivation, *XK*, like the gene for X-linked CGD, is subject to inactivation. A male patient with McLeod syndrome, CGD, Duchenne muscular dystrophy (DMD) and one type of retinitis pigmentosa (RP) was shown, both by DNA analysis and cytogenetics, to have an interstitial deletion of part of the short arm of the X chromosome at the Xp21.1 region[86] (Fig 1-3). Other patients, with smaller deletions at the same region, had McLeod syndrome and CGD but not DMD[87,89]; one also had RP.[88] This suggests that the *XK* locus is located at Xp21.1, very close to the genes for X-CGD (*CYBB*), DMD and RP (*RP3*). Bertelson et al[89] sited *XK* between the loci for CGD and DMD. It is known that X-linked CGD generally results from a deletion of part or all of the gene encoding cytochrome b-245, *CYBB*.[101] In some cases, the deletion must be large enough to encompass the *XK* gene as well, resulting in the McLeod phenotype.

Gerbich Negatives

Another depressed Kell phenotype resulting from inheritance of a rare gene at a separate locus is that accompanying some Gerbich-negative phenotypes. This phenomenon was first reported by Muller et al[102] in a woman and her brother with the rare GE:–2,–3 phenotype. Both showed weakened expression of KEL1, KEL2 and KEL4 antigens. In 1982 Daniels[103] reported that nine out of 11 red blood cell samples from GE:–2,–3 people showed at least some degree of weakening of Kell antigens: in some cases only KEL11 appeared to be affected, whereas in others all Kell antigens were depressed, although to a lesser extent than that found in the McLeod phenotype. All six GE:–2,3 samples had normal expression of Kell antigens.[103] Red blood cells of the GE:–2,–3,–4 Leach phenotype also demonstrated depression of at least some of the Kell system antigens.[104-106] Red blood cells with the K_o, K_{mod} and McLeod phenotypes and those with weakened expression of Kell antigens resulting from the *KEL 3/0* genotype (see below) have normal expression of Gerbich antigens.

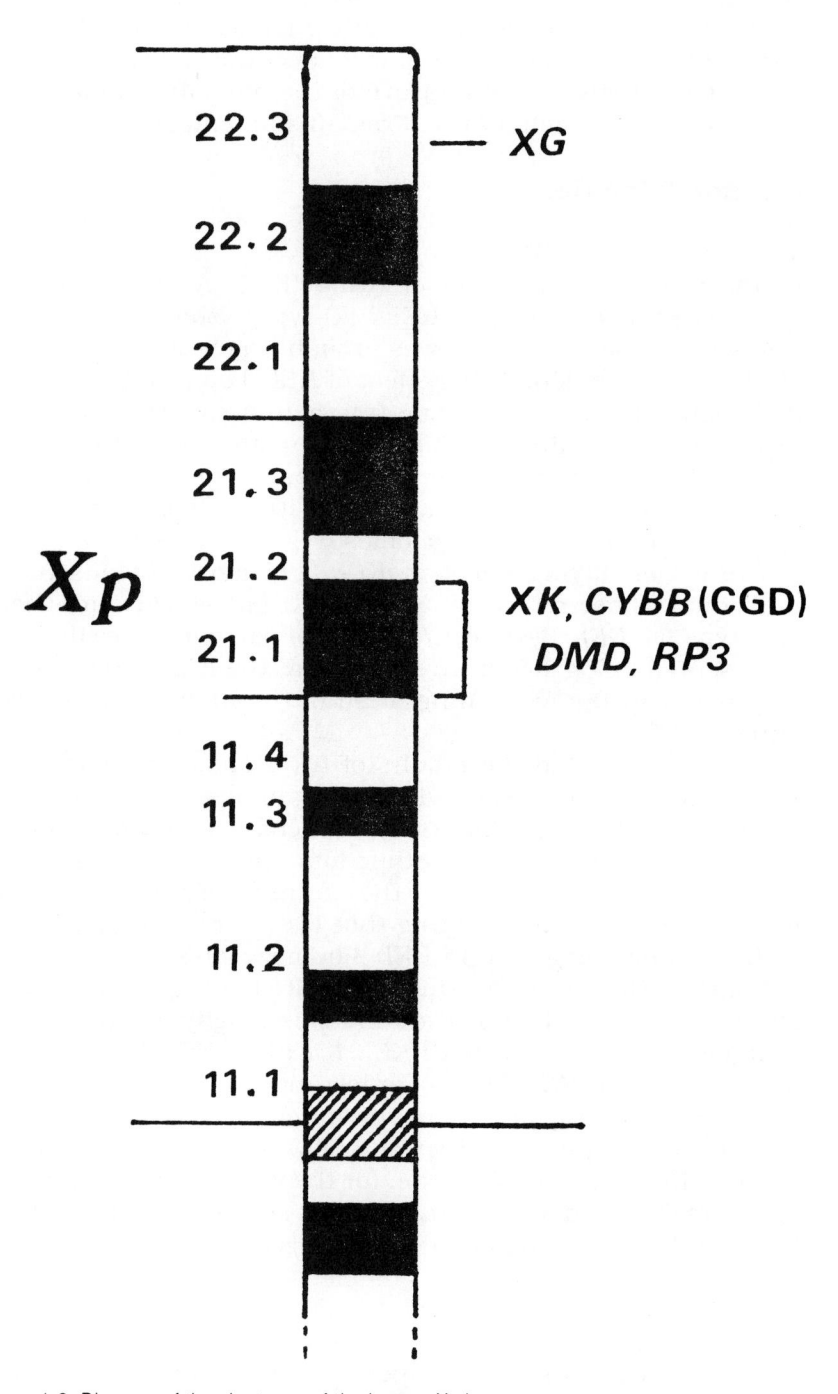

Figure 1-3. Diagram of the short arm of the human X chromosome.

Gerbich is genetically independent of Kell.[107] The biochemistry and molecular genetics of Gerbich are well understood: Gerbich-negative phenotypes result from deletions of different parts of the gene on chromosome 2 encoding glycophorin C.[108] However, the biochemical nature of the phenotypical association between Gerbich and Kell remains an enigma.

Cis Modifying Genes

In the original description of KEL3 (Kp^a), Allen and Lewis[6] reported some difficulty in KEL2 (k) typing some KEL:1,3 [K+ Kp(a+)] red blood cells. This was probably a result of weakening of KEL2 due to a depressing effect of *KEL 3* on *KEL 2* and other *KEL* genes in cis.[36] This gene interaction can only be recognized under certain conditions: when an alternative allele, such as *KEL 1*, is present on the opposite chromosome; when there is a *KEL 0* gene in trans; and, with difficulty, when *KEL 3* is present on both chromosomes (Fig 1-4).

The cis modifying effect of *KEL 3* is most obvious in an individual whose red blood cells are KEL:3,-4,-21 and whose genotype is *KEL 3/0 (Kp^a/K^0)*. Families, such as the one represented in Fig 1-5, have shown that the *KEL 3/0* genotype may result in the weakening of all of the high-incidence Kell antigens.[109,110]

Tippett[90] reported the results of titrations of selected anti-KEL2 and anti-KEL7 sera with five examples of KEL:3,-4 red blood cells. One gave markedly reduced scores and was assumed to be *KEL 3/0*; the other four, presumably *KEL 3/3*, showed a slight reduction in the strength of their KEL2 and KEL7 antigens, demonstrating that the cis modifying effect of *KEL 3* can be recognized in *KEL 3* homozygotes.

None of the other low-incidence Kell antigens has been shown to be weakened by the *KEL 3* cis modifying effect as no example of *KEL 3* in cis with *KEL 1, KEL 6, KEL 10* or *KEL 17* has been found. *KEL 21 (Kp^c)*, a low-incidence allele of *KEL 3*, does not apparently produce a similar effect when in trans with *KEL 0*.[48] If an epistatic effect of *KEL 3* on other *KEL* genes in cis were indeed the explanation for the weak expression of Kell and para-Kell antigens in *KEL 3/0*, as seems most likely, then the para-Kell antigens must be produced by genes at the *KEL* complex locus.

As described earlier, Marsh et al[21] proposed a similar cis modifying effect on *KEL* genes caused by a rare allele of the gene responsible for the production of KEL13 in a propositus and his sister whose red blood cells were KEL:-13.

Genotype   Diagrammatic representation   Phenotypic effect

                         depression of expression
                    3 ──▸2   other KEL genes
KEL 2,3/2,4   -------------------------------   No apparent
                    ---------------------------------   weakness
(kKp^a/kKp^b)   4   2   other KEL genes   of Kell antigens
                          no depression

                         depression of expression
                    3 ──▸2   other KEL genes
KEL 2,3/1,4   ---------------------------------   Only KEL2 shows
                    ---------------------------------   weakness
(kKp^a/KKp^b)   4   1   other KEL genes
                          no depression

                         depression of expression
                    3 ──▸2   other KEL genes
KEL 2,3/2,3   ---------------------------------   Some weakness of
                    ---------------------------------   Kell antigen
(kKp^a/kKp^a)   3 ──▸2   other KEL genes   (except KEL3)
                          depression of expression

                         depression of expression
                    3 ──▸2   other KEL genes
KEL 2,3/0   ---------------------------------   Weakness of
                    ---------------------------------   Kell antigens
(kKp^a/K^o)   0   (except KEL3)
                    No expression

Figure 1-4. Diagrammatic representation of the cis modifying effect of *KEL 3* on *KEL 2* and other *KEL* genes.

K$_{mod}$ Phenotype

Marsh and Redman[68] use K$_{mod}$ as an umbrella term to describe phenotypes in which Kell antigens are expressed only very weakly, often requiring adsorption/elution tests for detection, and in which Kx antigen expression is elevated.[111-114] The term K$_{mod}$ can be used to include phenotypes referred to as Day[111] and Mullins[112] in their original descriptions. Some individuals with the K$_{mod}$ phenotype may make an anti-KEL5-like antibody.[68,111,112,114]

K$_{mod}$ may be inherited, presumably as a recessive character, although this has not been confirmed. In a family described by Peloquin et al,[112] the aberrant phenotype (the Mullins phenotype) was detected in the propositus and in two of his four brothers but in none of his seven children and 13 grand-chil-

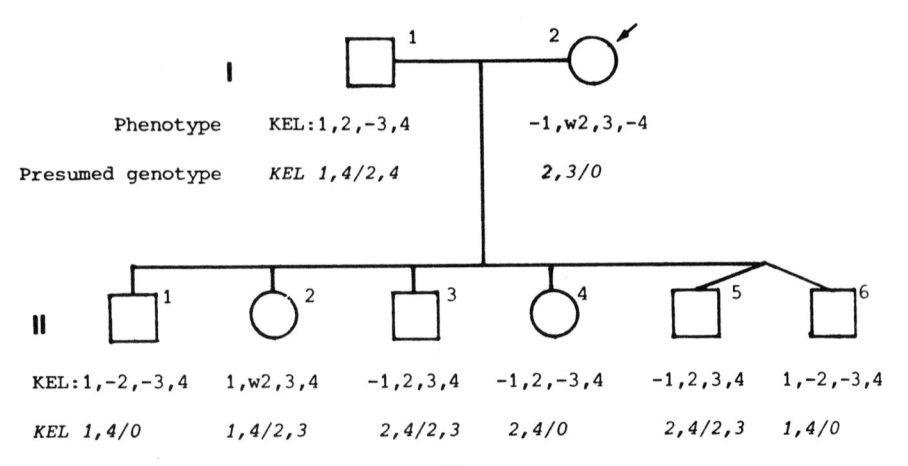

Figure 1-5. Family described by Walsh et al[110] demonstrating depressing effect of *KEL 3* on *KEL 2* in cis. Weakness of KEL2 antigen was apparent in I-2, who has a *KEL 0* gene, and in II-2, who has a *KEL 1* gene, in trans with *KEL 2*.

dren. A woman with the K_{mod} phenotype reported by Pehta et al[114] had a brother with a similar weak Kell phenotype. K_{mod} may be considered to be analogous to Rh_{mod} serologically, although the latter do not generally make Rh-specific antibodies. However, unlike Rh_{mod}, there is no evidence that K_{mod} results from homozygosity of a rare suppressor gene at an unlinked regulator locus.[115(p261)]

Allen Phenotype

The KEL:3,4 red blood cells of a blood donor and his sister demonstrated weak expression of their other Kell antigens and of KEL4. Their red blood cells reacted normally with anti-Kx + anti-KEL20 (anti-KL) serum. The KEL3 antigen expression appeared to be slightly enhanced compared with that of KEL: 3,4 control red blood cells. The new variant Kell phenotype was named the Allen phenotype.[116] A daughter of the propositus appeared to have inherited her father's *KEL 3* gene but her KEL4 and other Kell antigens were expressed normally. Red blood cells of the Allen phenotype siblings had both KEL3 and KEL4 antigens. Therefore, the siblings could not be of the *KEL 3/0* or *KEL 3/3* genotypes associated with Kell antigen depression due to a cis modifying effect (see above). The presence of the same rare phenotype in brother and sister suggests an inherited character, although the genetic background of the Allen phenotype remains unclear.

Acquired or Transient Depressed Kell Phenotypes

Although not strictly pertinent to the genetics of the Kell system, it should be mentioned here that some depressed Kell phenotypes may be acquired and possibly transient, with Kell antigen expression subsequently returning to normal. This effect has generally been associated with the presence of an autoantibody mimicking anti-KEL4[117-122] or an antibody to another high-incidence Kell antigen.[119] Degradation of Kell system antigens by enzymes of microbial origin has been proposed to explain this phenomenon.[118,119]

In a patient with a potent antibody to a high-incidence Kell antigen reported by Vengelen-Tyler et al,[123] the red blood cells gave a negative direct antiglobulin reaction and displayed profound depression of Kell system antigens. Transfused red blood cells also lost their Kell antigens. Five months after the original testing the antibody had disappeared and the patient's Kell antigens returned to normal. Again, an environmental agent, possibly of microbial origin, appeared to be responsible.

Genetic Linkage

Together with Diego, Yt and Dombrock, Kell is one of the few well-investigated blood group systems still awaiting chromosomal assignment. This is surprising as the frequency of KEL1 in Caucasian populations makes KEL1:2 (Kk) a useful polymorphism for family analysis and anti-KEL1 and anti-KEL2 are relatively plentiful and easy to use. Yet, not only has *KEL* not been assigned to a chromosome, only a very few other loci have been shown to be linked to it.

From an analysis of 31 families informative for segregation of *KEL* and the blood group locus *YT*, Coghlan et al[124] demonstrated loose linkage between these loci with maximum likelihood of a recombination fraction of 0.26 (26% recombination). Another gene that appears to be linked to *KEL* is that for the ability to taste phenylthiocarbamide (*PTC*). Although close linkage was found by Conneally et al,[125] previous and subsequent studies showed that only very loose linkage between *KEL* and *PTC* is likely.[126-129] *KEL*, *YT* and *PTC* make up unassigned linkage group (ULG) 1 (Tenth International Workshop on Human Gene Mapping, 1989[130]).

KEL has been excluded from over half of the human genetic linkage map.[129] Close linkage of KEL to a restriction fragment length polymorphism (RFLP) detected with a probe isolated from a chromosome 5 library suggested assignment of KEL to chromosome 5.[131] However, there was no linkage with other chromosome 5 markers and so the assignment remains unproven. There is also some evidence that YT, and therefore presumably KEL, may be located on the short arm of chromosome 6.[132] Tippett and Shaw[133] showed that KEL is not linked to XG. This may appear self-evident as Kell does not show an X-linked mode of inheritance. However, in the absence of any autosomal assignment of KEL, the remote possibility existed that KEL could be located on the pseudo-autosomal region at the telomere of the short arm of the X chromosome, in which case X-linkage would not be apparent because of crossing over with the Y chromosome.[96] As XG is situated close to this region of the X chromosome, pseudo-autosomal genes would probably be linked to XG.

In an attempt to end KEL's unassigned status, the Winnipeg group[124] is currently investigating linkage of KEL and YT with RFLPs that identify regions of the human genome from which these loci have not been excluded.

Evolutionary Aspects

Kell antigens may be restricted to erythroid cells. Parsons et al[134] showed, by flow cytometry, that several Kell-related monoclonal antibodies did not react with a number of hematopoietic cell lines or with human lymphocytes, granulocytes or unfractionated mononuclear cells. Cells of the human erythroleukemic line, K562, also did not express Kell antigens[134,135] unless induced to synthesize hemoglobin by hemin, after which KEL2, KEL4, KEL5 and KEL7 were detected.[135]

Two examples of monoclonal anti-KEL14 reacted with three samples each of chimpanzee, gorilla and gibbon red blood cells, but not with rhesus, baboon, duorocoli or squirrel monkey red blood cells.[136] Monoclonal anti-KEL2, however, reacted with all primate red blood cells tested.[136] Redman et al[137] found that chimpanzees (Pan troglodyte) have the Kell phenotype KEL: −1,2,−3,4,5,6,−7,11,12,13,14,18,19,22 Kx+. That is, the same as the common human Kell phenotype, except that the red blood cells of all 27 chimps tested were KEL:6,−7 [Js(a+b−)]. Furthermore, immunoprecipitation and immunoblotting revealed a close homology between human and chimp Kell glyco-protein, the latter probably having slightly more glycosylation. Redman et al[137] suggest that *KEL 6* may be the ancestral gene at this sublocus, *KEL 7* arising by mutation after the human and chimp evolutionary lines separated. This proposal con-flicts with that of Chown (cited in Issitt[115(p294)]) in which *KEL 2,4,7* represent ancestral *KEL* gene and *KEL 1*, *KEL 3* and *KEL 6* arose from separate mutations of *KEL 2*, *KEL 4* and *KEL 7* respectively, explaining why more than one of the lower inci-dence genes is never found in the same haplotype.

It seems likely that much may be learned from the great apes about the genetics and phylogeny of the Kell blood group system.

Conclusion

Kell is a complex blood group system. The wealth of serological knowledge pertinent to the Kell system has only led to a limited understanding of Kell genetics and there remain a number of unanswered questions. On which chromosome is the *KEL* gene located? Does the *KEL* gene really comprise a number of sub-loci or are there several very closely linked, but discrete, loci? Are the para-Kell antigens produced by genes at the *KEL* locus? How does the X-linked gene, *XK*, regulate expression of the *KEL* gene? Why is a *KEL* gene complex containing *KEL 3* expressed abnormally and how does the absence of GE3 anti-gen affect expression of Kell antigens? Hopefully, the answers to these questions will emerge from research into Kell genetics at the molecular level.

References

1. Lewis M, Anstee DJ, Bird GWG, et al. Terminology for red cell surface antigens. Vox Sang 1990;58:152-69.
2. Allen FH Jr, Rosenfield RE. Notation for the Kell blood-group system. Transfusion 1961;1:305-7.
3. Coombs RRA, Mourant AE, Race RR. In-vivo isosen-sitisation of red cells in babies with hemolytic disease. Lancet 1946;1:264-6.
4. Race RR. A summary of present knowledge of human blood-groups, with special reference to serological in-compatibility as a cause of congenital disease. Br Med Bull 1946;4:188-93.

5. Levine P, Backer M, Wigod M, Ponder R. A new human hereditary blood property (Cellano) present in 99.8% of all bloods. Science 1949;109:464-6.

6. Allen FH Jr, Lewis SJ. Kp^a (Penney), a new antigen in the Kell blood group system. Vox Sang 1957;2:81-7.

7. Allen FH Jr, Lewis SJ, Fudenburg H. Studies of anti-Kp^b, a new antibody in the Kell blood group system. Vox Sang 1958;3:1-13.

8. Corcoran PA, Allen FH Jr, Lewis M, Chown B. A new antibody, anti-Ku (anti-Peltz), in the Kell blood group system. Transfusion 1961;1:181-3.

9. Giblett ER. Js, a 'new' blood group antigen found in Negroes. Nature 1958;181:1221-2.

10. Giblett ER, Chase J. Js^a, a 'new' red-cell antigen found in Negroes; evidence for an eleventh blood group system. Br J Haematol 1959;5:319-26.

11. Stroup M, MacIlroy M, Walker R, Aydelotte JV. Evidence that Sutter belongs to the Kell blood group system. Transfusion 1965;5:309-14.

12. Walker RH, Argall CI, Steane EA, et al. Anti-Js^b, the expected antithetical antibody of the Sutter blood group system. Nature 1963;197:295-6.

13. Walker RH, Argall CI, Steane EA, et al. Js^b of the Sutter blood group system. Transfusion 1963;3:94-9.

14. Furuhjelm U, Nevanlinna HR, Nurkka R, et al. The blood group antigen Ul^a (Karhula). Vox Sang 1968;15:118-24.

15. Furuhjelm U, Nevanlinna HR, Nurkka R, et al. Evidence that the antigen Ul^a is controlled from the Kell complex locus. Vox Sang 1969;16:496-9.

16. Guévin RM, Taliano V, Waldmann O. The Côté serum (anti-K11), an antibody defining a new variant in the Kell system. Vox Sang 1976;31 suppl 1:96-100.

17. Sabo B, McCreary J, Gellerman M, et al. Confirmation of K^{11} and K^{17} as alleles in the Kell blood group system. Vox Sang 1975;29:450-5.

18. Heistø H, Guévin RM, Taliano V, et al. Three further antigen-antibody specificities associated with the Kell blood group system. Vox Sang 1973;24:179-80.

19. Marsh WL, Stroup M, MacIlroy M, et al. A new antibody, anti-K12, associated with the Kell blood group system. Vox Sang 1973;24:200-5.

20. Beattie KM, Heinz B, Korol S, et al. Anti-K12 in the serum of two brothers: Inheritance of the K:–12 phenotype. Rev Fr Transfus Immunohématol 1982;25:611-8.

21. Marsh WL, Jensen L, Øyen R, et al. Anti-K13 and the K:–13 phenotype. Vox Sang 1974;26:34-40.

22. Wallace ME, Bouysou C, de Jongh DS, et al. Anti-K14: An antibody specificity associated with the Kell blood group system. Vox Sang 1976;30:300-4.
23. Frank S, Schmidt RP, Baugh M. Three new antibodies to high-incidence antigenic determinants (anti-E1, anti-Dp, and anti-So). Transfusion 1970;10:254-7.
24. Sabo B, McCreary J, Harris P. Anti-Dp is anti-K14 (letter). Vox Sang 1982;43:56.
25. Marsh WL, Øyen R, Nichols ME, Allen FH Jr. Chronic granulomatous disease and the Kell blood groups. Br J Haematol 1975;29:247-62.
26. Strange JJ, Kenworthy RJ, Webb AJ, Giles CM. Wk^a (Weeks), a new antigen in the Kell blood group system. Vox Sang 1974;27:81-6.
27. Barrasso C, Eska P, Grindon AJ, et al. Anti-K18: An antibody defining another high-frequency antigen related to the Kell blood group system. Vox Sang 1975; 29:124-7.
28. Sabo B, McCreary J, Stroup M, et al. Another Kell-related antibody, anti-K19. Vox Sang 1979;36:97-102.
29. van der Hart M, Szaloky A, van Loghem JJ. A 'new' antibody associated with the Kell blood group system. Vox Sang 1968;15:456-8.
30. Marsh WL. Letter. Vox Sang 1979;36:375-6.
31. Yamaguchi H, Okubo Y, Seno T, et al. A 'new' allele, Kp^c, at the Kell complex locus. Vox Sang 1979;36:29-30.
32. Gavin J, Daniels GL, Yamaguchi H, et al. The red cell antigen once called Levay is the antigen Kp^c of the Kell system. Vox Sang 1979;36:31-3.
33. Bar Shany S, Ben Porath D, Levene C, et al. K22, a 'new' para-Kell antigen of high frequency. Vox Sang 1982; 42:87-90.
34. Marsh WL, Redman CM, Kessler LA, et al. K23 a low-incidence antigen in the Kell blood group system identified by biochemical characterization. Transfusion 1987;27: 36-40.
35. Eicher C, Kirkley K, Porter M, Kao Y. A new low frequency antigen in the Kell system: K24 (Cls) (abstract). Transfusion 1985;25:448.
36. Race RR, Sanger R. Blood groups in man. 6th ed. Oxford: Blackwell Scientific Publications, 1975.
37. Sanger R, Bertinshaw D, Lawler SD, Race RR. Les groupes sanguins humains Kell: Fréquences géniques et recherches génétiques. Rev d'Hemat 1949;4:32-5.

38. Lewis M, Chown B, Kaita H. Inheritance of blood group antigens in a largely Eskimo population sample. Am J Hum Genet 1963;15:203-8.
39. Lewis M, Kaita H, Chown B. The inheritance of the Kell blood groups in a Caucasian population sample. Vox Sang 1969;17:221-3.
40. Mourant AE, Kopec AC, Domaniewska-Sobczak K. The distribution of the human blood groups and other polymorphisms. 2nd ed. London: Oxford University Press, 1976.
41. Garretta M, Gener J, Muller A. Analyse de 280.000 déterminations du facteur Kell sur les équipments Groupamatic. Rev Fr Transfus Immunohematol 1978; 21:379-86.
42. Hamilton HB, Nakahara Y. The rare Kell blood group phenotype K^o in a Japanese family. Vox Sang 1971: 20:24-8.
43. Dichupa PJ, Anderson C, Chown B. A further search for hypothetic K^p of the Kell-system. Vox Sang 1969;17:1-4.
44. Chown B, Lewis M, Kaita H, Philipps S. Some blood group frequencies in a Caucasian population. Vox Sang 1963;8: 378-81.
45. Jarkowski TL, Hinshaw CP, Beattie KM, Silberberg B. Another example of anti-Js^a. Transfusion 1962;2:423-4.
46. Speilmann W, Teixidor D, Renninger W, Matznetter T. Blutgruppen und Lepra bei moçambiquanischen Völker schaften. Humangenetik 1970;10:304-17.
47. Okubo Y, Yamaguchi H, Seno T, et al. The first example of anti-Ul^a and Ul(a+) red cells found in Japan (letter). Transfusion 1986;26:215.
48. Kikuchi M, Endo N, Seno T, et al. A Japanese family with two Kp(a–b–c+) members, presumed genotype Kp^c/K^o. Transfusion 1983;23:254-5.
49. Kline WE, Sullivan CM, Bowman RJ. A rare example of weakened expression of the Kell (K1) antigen. Vox Sang 1984;47:170-3.
50. McDowell MA, Mann JM, Milakovic K. Kell-like antibody in a Kell positive patient (abstract). Transfusion 1978; 18:389.
51. McGinniss MH, MacLowry JD, Holland PV. Acquisition of K:1-like antigen during terminal sepsis. Transfusion 1984;24:28-30.
52. Lewis M, Kaita H, Duncan D, Chown B. Failure to find hypothetic K^a (KKp^a) of the Kell blood group system. Vox Sang 1960;5:565-7.

53. Wright J, Cornwall SM, Matsina E. A second example of hemolytic disease of the newborn due to anti-Kp[b]. Vox Sang 1965;10:218-21.

54. Callender S, Race RR, Paykoç ZV. Hypersensitivity to transfused blood. Br Med J 1945;2:83.

55. Callender ST, Race RR. A serological and genetical study of multiple antibodies formed in response to blood transfusion by a patient with lupus erythematosus diffusus. Ann Eugen 1946;13:102-17.

56. Daniels GL. Blood group antigens of high frequency: A serological and genetical study. PhD thesis, University of London, 1980.

57. Morton NE, Krieger H, Steinberg AG, Rosenfield RE. Genetic evidence confirming the localization of Sutter in the Kell blood-group system. Vox Sang 1965;10:608-13.

58. Ito K, Mukumoto Y, Konishi H. An example of 'naturally occurring' anti-Js[a] (K6) in a Japanese female. Vox Sang 1979;37:350-1.

59. Beattie KM, Shafer AW, Sigmund K, Cisco S. Mass screening of American Black donors to identify high incidence antigen-negative bloods (abstract). Proceedings of the 19th Congress of the International Society of Blood Transfusion Paris:ISBT, 1986.

60. Guévin RM, Taliano V, Waldman O. The Côté serum, an antibody defining a new variant in the Kell system (abstract). Program of the 24th Annual Meeting. Washington, DC: American Association of Blood Banks, 1971: 100.

61. Chown B, Lewis M, Kaita K. A 'new' Kell blood-group phenotype. Nature 1957;180:711.

62. Kaita H, Lewis M, Chown B, Gard E. A further example of the Kell blood group phenotype K-, k-, Kp(a-b-). Nature 1959;183:1586.

63. Chown B, Lewis M, Kaita H, et al. The pedigrees of two people already reported as of phenotype K-, k-, Kp(a-b-). Vox Sang 1961;6:620-3.

64. Nunn HD, Giles CM, Dormandy KM. A second example of anti-Ku in a patient who has the rare Kell phenotype, K[o]. Vox Sang 1966;11:611-9.

65. Marsh WL, Øyen R, Nichols ME. Kx antigen, the McLeod phenotype, and chronic granulomatous disease: Further studies. Vox Sang 1976;31:356-62.

66. Bradley PM, Henry H, Speake L. The occurrence of anti-Kp[b] alone in a patient of the K[o] phenotype (abstract). Proceedings of the 20th Congress of the International Society of Blood Transfusion. Paris: ISBT, 1988.

67. Marsh WL, Redman CM. Kell antigens and the McLeod red cell phenotype. In: Rouger P, Salmon C, eds. Monoclonal antibodies against human red blood cell and related antigens. Paris: Arnette Libraire, 1987:99-117.
68. Marsh WL, Redman CM. Recent developments in the Kell blood group system. Transfus Med Rev 1987;1:4-20.
69. Taylor HL. Anti-K12 in a Black? (letter). Transfusion 1979;19:787-8.
70. Marsh WL, DiNapoli J, Øyen R. Auto-immune hemolytic anemia caused by anti-K13. Vox Sang 1979;36:174-8.
71. Barrasso C, Baldwin ML, Drew H, Ness PM. In vivo survival of K:18 red cells in a recipient with anti-K18. Transfusion 1983;23:258-9.
72. Marsh WL, DiNapoli J, Øyen R, et al. Delayed hemolytic transfusion reaction caused by the second example of anti-K19. Transfusion 1979;19:604-8.
73. Manny N, Levene C, Harel N, et al. The second example of anti-K22 and a family genetically informative for K and K^{22}. Vox Sang 1985;49:135-7.
74. Marsh WL. Deleted antigens of the Rhesus and Kell blood groups: Association with cell membrane defects. In: Garratty G, ed. Blood group antigens and disease. Arlington, VA: American Association of Blood Banks, 1983: 165-85.
75. Allen FH Jr, Krabbe SMR, Corcoran PA. A new phenotype (McLeod) in the Kell blood-group system. Vox Sang 1961; 6:555-60.
76. Giblett ER, Klebanoff SJ, Pincus SH, et al. Kell phenotypes in chronic granulomatous disease: A potential transfusion hazard. Lancet 1971;1;1235-6.
77. Poole J. A new example of anti-KL. Med Lab Tech 1972; 29:62-5.
78. Brzica SM, Rhodes KH, Pineda AA, Taswell HF. Chronic granulomatous disease and the McLeod phenotype. Mayo Clin Proc 1977;52:153-6.
79. Bowell PJ, Hill FGH. Autoanalyzer determination of red cell Kell phenotypes in patients with chronic granulomatous disease (CGD) and heterozygous carriers. Br J Haematol 1978;39:351-5.
80. Symmans WA, Shepherd CS, Marsh WL, et al. Hereditary acanthocytosis associated with the McLeod phenotype of the Kell blood group system. Br J Haematol 1979;42:575-83.
81. White W, Washington ED, Sabo BH, et al. Anti-Km in a transfused man with McLeod syndrome. Rev Fr Transfus Immunohematol 1980;23:305-17.

82. Fikrig SM, Phillipp JCD, Smithwick EM, et al. Chronic granulomatous disease and McLeod syndrome in a Black child. Pediatrics 1980;66:403-4.
83. Marsh WL, Marsh NJ, Moore A, et al. Elevated serum creatine phosphokinase in subjects with McLeod syndrome. Vox Sang 1981;40:403-11.
84. Swash M, Schwartz MS, Carter ND, et al. Benign X-linked myopathy with acanthocytes (McLeod syndrome). Brain 1983;106:717-33.
85. Marsh WL, Schnipper EF, Johnson CL, et al. An individual with McLeod syndrome and the Kell blood group antigen K(K1). Transfusion 1983;23:336-8.
86. Francke U, Ochs HD, de Martinville D, et al. Minor Xp21 chromosome deletion in a male associated with expression of Duchenne muscular dystrophy, chronic gran-ulomatous disease, retinitis pigmentosa, and McLeod syndrome. Am J Hum Genet 1985;37:250-67.
87. Frey D, Mächler M, Seger R, et al. Gene deletion in a patient with chronic granulomatous disease and McLeod syndrome: Fine mapping of the Xk gene locus. Blood 1988;71:252-5.
88. de Saint-Basile G, Bohler MC, Fischer A, et al. Xp21 DNA microdeletion in a patient with chronic granulomatous disease, retinitis pigmentosa, and McLeod phenotype. Hum Genet 1988;80:85-9.
89. Bertelson CJ, Pogo AO, Chaudhuri A, et al. Localization of the McLeod locus (XK) within Xp21 by deletion analysis. Am J Hum Genet 1988;42:703-11.
90. Tippett P. Some recent developments in the Kell and Lutheran systems. In: Mohn JF, Plunkett RW, Cunningham RK, Lambert RM, eds. Human blood groups. Basel, Switzerland: Karger, 1977:401-9.
91. Advani H, Zamor J, Judd WJ, et al. Inactivation of Kell blood group antigens by 2-aminoethylisothiouronium bromide. Br J Haematol 1982;51:107-15.
92. Sharp D, Rogers S, Dickstein B, et al. Successful transfusion of K_o blood to a Km–Kx– patient with anti-Km (abstract). Transfusion 1988;28, suppl:37S.
93. Sullivan CM, Kline WE, Rabin BI, et al. The first example of autoanti-Kx. Transfusion 1987;27:322-4.
94. Segal AW. Variations on the theme of chronic gran-ulomatous disease. Lancet 1985;1:1378-83.
95. Lyon MF. X-chromosome inactivation and developmental patterns in mammals. Biol Rev 1972;47:1-35.

96. Burgoyne PS. Genetic homology and crossing over in the X and Y chromosomes of mammals. Hum Genet 1982; 61:85-90.

97. Marsh WL, Taswell HF, Øyen R, et al. Kx antigen of the Kell system and its relationship to chronic granulo-matous disease. Evidence that the Kx gene is X-linked (abstract). Transfusion 1975;15:527.

98. Wimer BM, Marsh WL, Taswell HF, Galey WR. Haematological changes associated with the McLeod phenotype of the Kell blood group system. Br J Haematol 1977; 36:219-24.

99. Marsh WL. Linkage relationship of the *Xg* and *Xk* loci. Human gene mapping 4. Cytogenet Cell Genet 1978; 22:531-3.

100. Wolff G, Müller CR, Jobke A. Linkage of genes for chronic granulomatous disease and Xg. Hum Genet 1980;54: 269-71.

101. Orkin SH. X-linked chronic granulomatous disease: from chromosomal position to the *in vivo* gene product. Trends Genet 1987;3:149-51.

102. Muller A, André-Liardet J, Garretta M, et al. Observations sur un anticorps rare: l'anti-Gerbich. Rev Fr Transfus Immunohematol 1973;16:251-7.

103. Daniels GL. Studies on Gerbich negative phenotypes and Gerbich antibodies (abstract). Transfusion 1982;22:405.

104. Anstee DJ, Ridgwell K, Tanner MJA, et al. Individuals lacking the Gerbich blood-group antigen have alterations in the human erythrocyte membrane sialoglycoproteins β and γ. Biochem J 1984;221:97-104.

105. Daniels GL, Shaw MA, Judson PA, et al. A family demonstrating inheritance of the Leach phenotype: A Gerbich-negative phenotype associated with elliptocytosis. Vox Sang 1986;50:117-21.

106. McShane K, Chung A. A novel human alloantibody in the Gerbich system. Vox Sang 1989;57:205-9.

107. Rosenfield RE, Haber GV, Kissmeyer-Nielson F, et al. Ge, a very common red-cell antigen. Br J Haematol 1960; 6:344-9.

108. Reid ME. Biochemistry and molecular cloning analysis of human red cell sialoglycoproteins that carry Gerbich blood group antigens. In: Unger P, Laird-Fryer B, eds. Blood group systems: MN and Gerbich. Arlington, VA: American Association of Blood Banks, 1989:73-103.

109. Ford DS, Knight AE, Smith F. A further example of Kp^a/K^o exhibiting depression of some Kell group antigens. Vox Sang 1977;32:220-3.

110. Walsh TJ, Daniels GL, Tippett P. A family with unusual Kell genotypes. Forensic Sci Int 1981;18:161-3.
111. Brown A, Berger R, Lasko D, et al. The Day phenotype: a 'new' variant in the Kell blood group system. Rev Fr Transfus Immunohematol 1982;25:619-27.
112. Peloquin P, Yochum G, Hagy L, et al. The Mullins phenotype: Another RBC phenotype characterized by weak Kell antigens (abstract). Transfusion 1988;28, suppl: 19S.
113. Winkler MM, Beattie KM, Cisco SL, et al. The K_{mod} blood group phenotype in a healthy individual. Transfusion 1989;29:642-5.
114. Pehta JC, Johnson CL, Giller RL, et al. Evidence that K_{mod} is an inherited condition (abstract). Transfusion 1989; 29,suppl:15S.
115. Issitt PD. Applied blood group serology. 3rd ed. Miami: Montgomery Scientific Publications, 1985.
116. Norman PC, Daniels GL. Unusual suppression of Kell system antigens in a healthy blood donor. Transfusion 1988;28:460-2.
117. Seyfried H, Górska B, Maj S, et al. Apparent depression of antigens of the Kell blood group system associated with autoimmune acquired haemolytic anaemia. Vox Sang 1972;23:528-36.
118. Beck ML, Marsh WL, Pierce SR, et al. Auto-anti-Kp[b] associated with weakened antigenicity in the Kell blood group system: A second example. Transfusion 1979; 19:197-202.
119. Marsh WL, Øyen R, Alicea E, et al. Autoimmune hemolytic anemia and the Kell blood groups. Am J Hematol 1979;7:155-62.
120. Manny N, Levene C, Sela R, et al. Autoimmunity and the Kell blood groups: Auto-anti-Kp[b] in a Kp(a+b–) patient. Vox Sang 1983;45:252-6.
121. Brendel WL, Issitt PD, Moore RE, et al. Temporary reduction of red cell Kell system antigen expression and transient production of anti-Kp[b] in a surgical patient. Biotest Bull 1985;2:201-6.
122. Puig N, Carbonell F, Marty ML. Another example of mimicking anti-Kp[b] in a Kp(a+b–) patient. Vox Sang 1986;51:57-9.
123. Vengelen-Tyler V, Gonzalez B, Garratty G, et al. Acquired loss of red cell Kell antigens. Br J Haematol 1987;65:231-4.

124. Coghlan G, Kaita H, Belcher E, et al. Evidence for genetic linkage between the *KEL* and *YT* blood group loci. Vox Sang 1989;57:88-9.

125. Conneally PM, Dumont-Driscoll M, Huntzinger RS, et al. Linkage relations of the loci for Kell and phenylthiocarbamide taste sensitivity. Hum Hered 1976;26:267-71.

126. Umansky I, Reid J, Corcoran PA, et al. Genetics of blood groups. Linkage analysis of 207 pedigrees. Vox Sang 1966;11:450-9.

127. Spence MA, Falk CT, Neiswanger K, et al. Estimating the recombination frequency for the PTC-Kell linkage. Hum Genet 1984;67:183-6.

128. Crandall BF, Spence MA. Linkage relations of the phenylthiocarbamide locus (PTC). Hum Hered 1974;24:247-52.

129. Farre LA, Spence MA, Bonne-Tamir B, et al. Evidence for exclusion of the Kell blood group (KEL) from more than one-half of the human genetic linkage map. Human gene mapping 9 (abstract). Cytogenet Cell Genet 1987;46:613.

130. Keats B, Ott J, Conneally M. Report of the committee on linkage and gene order. Human gene mapping 10. Cytogenet Cell Genet 1989;51:459-502.

131. Leppert M, Wasmuth J, Overhauser J, et al. A primary linkage map of chromosome 5. Human gene mapping 9 (abstract). Cytogenet Cell Genet 1987;46:649.

132. Lewis M, Kaita H, Philipps S, et al. The Yt blood group system (ISBT no. 011). Genetic studies. Vox Sang 1987; 53:52-6.

133. Tippett P, Shaw MA. Are any unassigned blood group loci X-borne? Human Gene Mapping 7 (abstract). Cytogenet Cell Genet 1984;38:596-7.

134. Parsons SF, Judson PA, Spring FA, et al. Antibodies with specificities related to the Kell blood group system. 1st international workshop on monoclonal antibodies against human red blood cell and related antigens. Rev Fr Transfus Immunohematol 1988;31:401-5.

135. McGiniss MH, Dean A. Expression of red cell antigens by K562 human leukemia cells before and after induction of hemoglobin synthesis by hemin. Transfusion 1985;25:105-9.

136. Nichols ME, Rosenfield RE, Rubenstein P. Monoclonal anti-K14 and anti-K2. Vox Sang 1987;52:231-5.

137. Redman CM, Lee S, Ten Bokkel Huinink D, et al. Comparison of human and chimpanzee Kell blood group systems. Transfusion 1989;29:486-90.

In: Laird-Fryer B, Daniels G and Levitt J, eds.
Blood Group Systems: Kell
Arlington, VA: American Association
of Blood Banks, 1990

2

Serology and Clinical Significance of Kell Blood Group System Antibodies

Maxine H. Schultz, MA, MT(ASCP)SBB

TO DATE, 21 ANTIBODIES DIRECTED against Kell blood group system antigens have been identified. This chapter serves to review these antibody specificities and to present information regarding their sources of stimulation, clinical significance and serological characteristics.

Antibody Specificities

The Kell blood group system nomenclature as established by the International Society of Blood Transfusion (ISBT) Working Party on Terminology for Red Cell Surface Antigens has been introduced in Chapter 1. References to articles describing the antigen discoveries are also listed in that chapter.

Eight Kell blood group system antibodies detect low-incidence red blood cell antigens: KEL1 (K), KEL3 (Kp[a]), KEL6 (Js[a]), KEL10 (Ul[a]), KEL17 (Wk[a]), KEL21 (Kp[c]), KEL23 and KEL24. Thirteen antibodies detect high-incidence red blood cell antigens: KEL2 (k), KEL4 (Kp[b]), KEL5 (Ku), KEL7 (Js[b]), KEL11, KEL12, KEL13, KEL14, KEL16, KEL18, KEL19, KEL20 (Km) and KEL22. Three antigens—KEL8 (K[W]), KEL9 (KL) and KEL15 (Kx)—are now considered obsolete. Anti-KL was originally found in the serum of Claas, a young male whose red blood

Maxine H. Schultz, MA, MT(ASCP)SBB, Director, Consultation and Reference Laboratory, Gulf Coast Regional Blood Center, Houston, Texas cells exhibited the McLeod phenotype. Subsequent adsorption studies showed this serum to contain separable antibodies directed against KEL20 and Kx, the antigen produced by the *XK* gene described in Chapter 1.

Antibodies Directed Against Antigens Controlled at the *KEL* Locus

The four sets of alleles that have been shown to reside at the *KEL* complex locus are as follows: *KEL 1* and *KEL 2*; *KEL 3*, *KEL 4* and *KEL 21*; *KEL 6* and *KEL 7*; *KEL 11* and *KEL 17*. The *KEL 10* allele has also been shown to reside at the *KEL* locus; however, the antithetical partner has not yet been identified.

Examples of apparent alloanti-KEL1 and alloanti-KEL7 in the sera of patients whose red blood cells are phenotypically KEL:1 and KEL:6,7, respectively, suggest the possibility that a mosaic situation may exist similar to that found in other blood group systems.[1,2]

Antibodies Defining Para-Kell Antigens

The para-Kell antigens—KEL12, KEL13, KEL14, KEL18, KEL19, KEL22, KEL23 and KEL24—have not yet been shown to be genetically controlled from the *KEL* locus, but a phenotypic association with Kell system antigens can be deduced. These antigens are not detectable on K_o red blood cells and are only weakly expressed on red blood cells of the McLeod phenotype. Red blood cells lacking these para-Kell antigens may display a weakened KEL4 antigen. Also, even without family studies proving genetical linkage with the Kell system, biochemical studies showing that these antigens are present on the Kell glycoprotein suggest that they are probably controlled by genes at the *KEL* locus.

Monoclonal Antibodies

In 1982, Parsons et al[3] described a mouse monoclonal antibody (MoAb), BRIC 18, that demonstrated Kell-related specificity. This IgG2a antibody did not react with K_o red blood cells and reacted only weakly with McLeod phenotype red blood cells. The antigen detected by this antibody was destroyed by treatment with 2-aminoethylisothiouronium bromide (AET), but was not affected by treatment with trypsin or chymotrypsin either sequentially or in combination—a technique known to inactivate the KEL1 antigen.

Five years later, Nichols et al[4] reported a MoAb with anti-KEL14 specificity and one with anti-KEL2 specificity. These IgG1 antibodies were serologically similar to human antibodies and did not react with AET-treated red blood cells. In tests with the MoAbs, the KEL14 antigen was detected on red blood cells of the great apes (chimp, gorilla and gibbon), but not on the red blood cells of the rhesus monkey, baboon, dourocoli monkey or squirrel. The KEL2 antigen, however, was detected on all primate red blood cells. Sonneborn et al[5] reported further testing on a MoAb specific for the KEL2 (k) antigen.

In 1988, five MoAbs showing serological specificity within the Kell blood group system were distributed to eight laboratories participating in the First International Workshop on Monoclonal Antibodies against Human Red Cell and Related Antigens.[6-12] All of these antibodies were shown to be nonreactive with K_o red blood cells and with AET-treated red blood cells of common Kell phenotypes. A human MoAb, 26W12, showed anti-KEL1 specificity, but was found to be nonreactive with red blood cells from a family whose red blood cells expressed weak KEL1 antigens, as detected with polyclonal reagents. This MoAb has the potential, however, to be an effective blood grouping reagent because its human origin allows the use of routine antihuman globulin (AHG) reagents and because only one wash is necessary prior to the addition of AHG due to its supernatant origin.

The murine MoAbs, 20W3 and 20W4, which demonstrate anti-KEL14 and anti-KEL2 specificity respectively, are the same antibodies as those reported by Nichols et al.[4] The other two antibodies, 19W2 and 9W12, surely recognize high-incidence antigens related to the Kell blood group system, although different laboratories evaluating these antibodies were not in total agreement as to the exact specificities detected. None of the antibodies react by Western immunoblotting techniques, but biochemical studies using an immunoprecipitation technique show that three of the antibodies react with an epitope on the Kell 93,000-dalton glycoprotein.[6-12]

Autoantibody Specificities

Approximately one in 170 patients with ongoing warm autoimmune processes has an IgG autoantibody with specificity related to the Kell blood group system. Approximately 75% of these patients also have alloanti-KEL1 in their sera.[13] Usually, the relationship of the autoantibody to the Kell blood group system is manifested only by the nonreactivity of the serum or eluate with K_o or AET-treated red blood cells. Sometimes, however, the antibody demonstrates a clear-cut specificity, such as anti-KEL1 (-K),[14,15] anti-KEL4 (-Kp^b),[16-18] or anti-KEL13.[19] Unlike traditional autoantibodies, which are recovered from antigen-positive red blood cells, many of these autoantibodies appear to be specific for an antigen that the patient's red blood cells lack (eg, apparent anti-KEL1 may be seen in the eluate of a nontransfused individual whose red blood cells are phenotypically KEL:–1). Not infrequently, the autoantibody will react more strongly with red blood cells possessing a certain Kell antigen, but will still react with red blood cells lacking that antigen. This "mimicking" phenomenon has been reported with autoantibodies directed against antigens of other blood group systems, such as the Rh system.[20] In such cases, one can at least partially remove the autoantibody activity by multiple adsorptions with apparently antigen-negative red blood cells of common Kell phenotypes.[21,22]

Anti-KEL1 or anti-KEL1-like antibodies appear as the most commonly reported specificities. Issitt[23] notes that many patients with autoanti-KEL1 have suffered head injuries or have brain tumors, and he hypothesizes that damaged brain tissue might trigger autoantibody production.

Approximately half of the cases of Kell-related autoantibodies involve a transient depression of Kell blood group system antigens.[24,25] Other blood group antigens do not appear affected. Sometimes the antigen becomes so weakened that the autoantibody is first thought to be allo in nature. It is thought that the weakened antigen status of the patient's red blood cells might confer some protection from destruction by the autoantibody.

Seyfried et al[24] described the case of a 17-year-old male whose serum contained anti-KEL4, which caused severe hemolytic anemia. During the acute phase, his antibody did not appear to react with his own red blood cells; however, his own red blood cells and KEL:4 red blood cells had shortened survival. Transfusion of KEL:–4 red blood cells was necessary to relieve his anemia. Sixteen weeks later, when the antibody disappeared from the patient's serum, the expression of the patient's Kell system red blood cell antigens returned to normal. Throughout convalescence, the patient's direct antiglobulin test (DAT) was weakly positive due to complement, but 18 months later there were no symptoms of hemolytic anemia.

Beck et al[16] reported the second case of autoanti-KEL4 in a patient with weakened Kell system antigens. The autoantibody had high avidity for random red blood cells, but low avidity for the patient's own red blood cells. The DAT was positive with both anti-IgG and anti-C3 reagents. This patient had a lesion of the intestinal tract, and the authors suggested that this lesion facilitated absorption of bacterial growth products, which stimulated autoantibody formation.

Two mechanisms for the weakened antigens have been proposed. First is the possibility that bacterial or viral enzymes alter the antigens by removing Kell-specific sugars from the red blood cell membrane. A second possibility is that an unknown factor prevents the expression or synthesis of Kell system antigens.

Clinical Significance of Kell Blood Group System Antibodies

Risk of Alloimmunization

Before Rh immune globulin therapy became routine care for the Rh negative obstetrical patient, anti-RH1 (-D) was the most commonly identified alloantibody. As preventive medicine by-passed the stimulus for anti-RH1 production, the proportion of other Rh antibodies and anti-KEL1 has risen. Mollison[26] states that Kell antibodies comprise two-thirds of all antibodies identified outside of the ABO and Rh blood group systems. Evaluation of cases of patients presenting with anti-RH4 (-c) or anti-KEL1 reveals that the stimulus for antibody production is more likely to be pregnancy in the case of anti-RH4 and transfusion in the case of anti-KEL1.[27] The probability that a patient whose red blood cells are phenotypically KEL:–1 will produce anti-KEL1 upon receipt of one unit of KEL:1 red blood cells is one in 10. Therefore, the KEL1 antigen appears to be at least six times less immunogenic than the RH1 antigen.[28] Giblett[29] further notes that the immunogenicity of KEL1 is 2.5 times greater than RH4, three times greater than RH3 (E), and at least 20 times greater than any other major blood group antigen. Although the clinical significance of anti-KEL1 is undisputed, the low likelihood of antibody formation does not justify providing KEL:–1 red blood cells for all patients whose red blood cells are KEL:–1.

Immunoglobulin Classes and Sources of Antibody Stimulation

Most examples of Kell blood group system antibodies are red blood cell-stimulated IgG immunoglobulins. Approximately

20% of anti-KEL1 antibodies will bind complement; however, intravascular hemolysis due to anti-KEL1 or anti-KEL2 is rare.[30]

Several investigators have shown that IgG1 is the predominant IgG subclass of Kell antibodies.[31-33] Hunt et al[31] examined eight examples of anti-KEL1. All contained IgG1, and four also contained lesser amounts of IgG4. Michaelson and Kornstad[32] studied 20 examples of anti-KEL1. IgG1 was present in all samples, but 50% of the antibodies also contained IgG4. Additionally, these researchers found three of the 20 antibodies to contain an IgG3 component.

Hopkins et al[34] examined 18 examples of anti-KEL1 and three examples of anti-KEL2 that agglutinated antigen-positive red blood cells in saline. Using DEAE-Sephadex A-50 columns, they demonstrated that 12 out of 18 anti-KEL1 samples contained an IgG component, while IgM immunoglobulin was also present in nine samples. It was noted that recent transfusion correlated somewhat with the presence of IgM, but that the time factor was not the sole determinant affecting the ratio of IgM to IgG.

The existence of IgM saline-reactive anti-KEL1 has long been recognized. Morgan and Bossom[35] reported finding saline-reactive anti-KEL1 in the sera of two nontransfused adult males. No explanation was given for this reactivity. Mukumoto et al[36] also identified an IgM anti-KEL1 in the serum of a nontransfused male; again, no explanation was presented.

A few years later, Tegoli et al[37] reported another low titer anti-KEL1 detectable at room temperature and 37 C, but not in the AHG phase. Reactivity was abolished by treating the serum with 2-mercaptoethanol (2-ME); hence the conclusion that the antibody was an IgM immunoglobulin. The patient was a nontransfused male with lymphosarcoma and pulmonary tuberculosis. Subsequent reports of IgM anti-KEL1 antibodies have also noted possible associations with bacterial infections. In 1978, Marsh et al[38] investigated a 20-day-old nontransfused infant with acute *Escherichia coli* enterocolitis due to an uncommon B-variant pathogenic coliform. Testing revealed low titer, but high avidity anti-A and anti-KEL1 that reacted optimally at room temperature. The antibodies were not of maternal origin; the mother was a group A individual with no anti-KEL1 detectable in her serum. When additional testing was performed on the healthy infant at 14 weeks of age, the antibodies were no longer detectable. Cell-free preparations made from broth cultures of the causative organism *E. coli* 0125:B15 were proven to possess A-like and KEL1-like antigens by their ability to inhibit IgM anti-A and anti-KEL1. The culture media could not, however, convert KEL:–1 red blood cells to KEL:1. It was suggested that bacterial metabolites having A-like and KEL:1-like antigens were absorbed through the infant's intestinal tract and stimulated IgM antibody production.

Later reports of "naturally occurring" anti-KEL1 antibodies implicated mycobacterium,[39] *Streptococcus faecium*,[40] *Morganella morganii*,[41] an unidentified viral agent causing an upper respiratory infection[42] and other unidentified bacteria.[43]

In 1988, Savalonis et al[44] reported testing 23 gram-negative bacteria for the presence of KEL1-like antigens by hemagglutination inhibition techniques using IgG and IgM examples of anti-KEL1. Testing included saline-suspended whole organisms, cell-free culture media, and disrupted (sonicated) organisms, representing the following 10 genera: *Citrobacter*, *Edwardsiella*, *Enterobacter*, *Escherichia*, *Klebsiella*, *Proteus*, *Pseudomonas*, *Salmonella*, *Serratia* and *Shigella*. Testing involved incubating 0.5 mL anti-KEL1 with 0.5 mL test solution before adding KEL:1 indicator red blood cells. When IgM anti-KEL1 was used, the testing involved a 30-minute room temperature incubation. When IgG anti-Kell was used, testing was performed by a 37 C AHG (IgG) technique. Doubling dilutions of the antibody were used, and blank dilution controls were run in parallel. A two-tube difference between the dilution control and the test was interpreted as inhibition. *E. coli* 0125:B15, subtype 12808 was capable of inhibiting IgM anti-KEL1, but not the IgG form. Only the disrupted organisms exhibited this KEL1-like antigenicity, implying that the responsible structure is cryptic and not readily accessible in the intact bacteria. An isolate of *Shigella sonnei* was shown to inhibit anti-KEL1, but inhibition was not specific; IgG anti-KEL4, anti-FY1 (-Fy^a), anti-MNS3 (-S) and anti-RH4 (-c) were inhibited also.

Anti-KEL1 is not the only antibody specificity within the Kell blood group system to have been found as an IgM immunoglobulin. Several examples of anti-KEL2 (-k) reacting optimally in room temperature saline testing have been cited in the literature.[45-47] Ito et al[48] reported an example of a naturally occurring anti-KEL6 (-Js^a) in a Japanese female who had never been transfused and whose children's red blood cells were phenotypically KEL:–6. The antibody reacted at 22 C in saline and low ionic strength saline (LISS) solutions, at ficin 37 C, and in AHG testing using polyspecific AHG. Destruction of reactivity by treatment of the serum with 2-ME indicated the IgM nature of the antibody.

Hemolytic Disease of the Newborn

Two critical elements that combine to cause hemolytic disease of the newborn (HDN) are early antigenic development and the presence of corresponding maternal IgG antibodies. The KEL1 antigen has been shown to be well developed by 10 weeks gestation, while the KEL2 antigen is well developed by 6-7 weeks. The KEL3 (Kp[a]) antigen has been detected in a 16-week-old fetus. The KEL6 (Js[a]) antigen can be detected in a 19-week-old fetus and is well developed, along with KEL4 (Kp[b]) and KEL7 (Js[b]) at birth.[49] As has been discussed in a previous section, most antibodies directed against Kell blood group system antigens are IgG immunoglobulins, which are capable of crossing the placenta to cause HDN.

It has been noted that only 2% of HDN cases are due to antibodies other than those directed against ABO or Rh antigens.[50] Antibodies causing Rh-related HDN are most often stimulated by pregnancy alone, but non-Rh antibodies causing HDN are most often stimulated by transfusion. Hardy and Napier[51] note that HDN due to non-Rh antibodies is generally not as severe as that caused by Rh antibodies. They report that 96.1% of infants born to Rh-negative mothers with anti-RH1 (D) have a positive DAT, while only 45.9% of infants born to mothers with non-Rh antibodies have a positive DAT. Forty-two percent of infants suffering from HDN due to anti-RH1 require transfusion, while only 14% of at risk infants suffering from HDN due to other antibodies require transfusion. Most antibodies directed against Kell blood group system antigens cause a relatively mild form of HDN with anti-KEL1 proving the exception to the rule.

Pepperel et al[52] reviewed obstetrical records in Melbourne, Australia from 1965 through 1975. After examining cases of HDN due to Rh, KEL1, KEL2, MNS1 (M) and Duffy antibodies, they concluded that only cases involving Rh or KEL1 antibodies required exchange transfusions or resulted in perinatal demise. They reported 32 patients with anti-KEL1. Twenty-six of these women had a history of transfusion. In most cases, the infants delivered had red blood cells that were phenotypically KEL:-1 and were unaffected by the maternal antibody. Only two of those 26 women gave birth to infants whose red blood cells were KEL:1. The infants' red blood cells exhibited a positive DAT, but no transfusion was needed. In the remaining six patients, the outcome was not so benign. Five cord blood samples from women immunized by pregnancy alone exhibited a positive DAT; one stillbirth occurred, two infants were hydropic and were treated with exchange transfusion before expiring and two others expired within the neonatal period. The investigators concluded that all infants with severe HDN due to anti-KEL1 were born to mothers immunized through pregnancy alone. In these situations, repeated stimulation by multiple pregnancies and at least a 50% chance of having a fetus with red blood cells phenotypically KEL:1 were thought to increase the likelihood of severe HDN.

Wenk et al[53] noted that although examples of anti-KEL1 are approximately 60% as frequent as anti-RH1, anti-KEL1 causes only 3% as many cases of HDN as does anti-RH1. These investigators explained this discrepancy by the relatively low probability of the father's red blood cells being KEL:1 and by the relatively high incidence of transfusion-induced alloimmunization. They report severe HDN due to anti-KEL1 in 50% of cases; 50% of HDN cases due to anti-KEL1 require no transfusion therapy. It was also noted that titers of maternal antibody do not always predict severity of HDN. In one case, a titer of 128 was associated with mild HDN, while in another case, the same titer was associated with severe HDN. Similarly, an earlier report by Leventhal and Wolf[54] documented a stillbirth due to anti-KEL1 with an AHG titer of only 64.

Several recommendations can be advanced for proper management of the obstetrical patient who is phenotypically KEL: –1. The first step is the easiest, but often most disregarded tool of management—the performance of an antibody screen on all obstetrical patients, regardless of their Rh type. If anti-KEL1 is identified in the patient's serum, phenotyping the father's red blood cells for the KEL1 and KEL2 antigens will determine the likelihood of the fetal red blood cells being KEL:1. Periodic titration of the patient's antibody should be performed; however, as stated above, a low titer or a titer that does not increase significantly may give a false sense of security. Other recommended antenatal procedures include: 1) amniocentesis for an evaluation of the lecithin/sphingomyelin (L/S) ratio to determine fetal maturity and to determine the need for exchange transfusion and 2) chorionic villi sampling between the 8th and 11th week of gestation to obtain fetal red blood cells for antigen typing. If the fetus is found to lack the antigen in question, the physician can immediately allay the fears of the patient and her family regarding the outcome of the pregnancy, as well as remove the need for further risky diagnostic procedures.[55,56]

At least one report exists of a transfusion-induced anti-KEL2 causing severe HDN. The antibody was identified during the patient's first pregnancy. This first child was delivered at 37 weeks' gestation and required a partial exchange transfusion. Serial amniotic fluid measurements during the second pregnancy, however, indicated fetal distress at 30 weeks' gestation. Although the maternal antibody titer was only 16, fetal blood sampling was performed. The fetal red blood cells appeared to be KEL:1,2 and exhibited a weakly positive DAT. Hemoglobin and bilirubin results indicated severe erythroblastosis. Therefore, three intrauterine transfusions were given to support the fetus to maturity. A healthy infant was delivered at 36 weeks, 5 days with 96.5% of his red blood cells determined to be KEL:1,-2. No neonatal exchange transfusion was necessary. This case prompted these Canadian investigators to review records from the previous 20-year period. Out of 3426 instances of antibodies in 175,000 obstetrical patients, only 348 (10%) were anti-KEL1 and one (0.03%) was anti-KEL2. In this last case of HDN due to anti-KEL2, the woman was transfused 18 years prior to becoming pregnant with twins whose red blood cells were found to be KEL:2. From the 9th-36th week of gestation, the maternal antibody titer was reported as 8. At delivery, the twins' red blood cells exhibited strongly positive DATs. Simple transfusions were performed in the neonatal period; exchange transfusions were not required. The authors emphasize that unusually low titers of anti-KEL1 (-K) and anti-KEL2 (-k) can cause severe HDN.[57]

Other reports of HDN due to anti-KEL3 (-Kp[a]),[58] anti-KEL4 (-Kp[b]),[59,60] anti-KEL5 (-Ku),[61] anti-KEL6 (-Js[a]),[62,63] anti-KEL7 (-Js[b]),[64,65] anti-KEL14,[66] anti-KEL22[67,68] and anti-KEL23[69] indicate that Kell blood group system antibodies usually cause mild HDN. The red blood cells of the newborn infant may demonstrate a strongly positive DAT, but the infant generally exhibits mild clinical signs of HDN and rarely requires transfusion therapy.

Significance of Kell Blood Group System Antibodies in Transfusion Therapy

Within a few years of identifying the KEL1 antigen, a case of a fatal transfusion reaction due to anti-KEL1 was reported by Ottensooser et al.[70] The patient received 500 mL of KEL:1 blood that had not been crossmatched. A severe hemolytic reaction ensued, culminating in death 8 days posttransfusion. Anti-KEL1 produced in response to transfusion 23 years earlier was identified as the cause for the hemolysis.

Anti-KEL1 present in donor plasma has also been implicated in hemolytic transfusion reactions in patients whose red blood cells are phenotypically KEL:-1 and who have received KEL:1

red blood cells. Zettner and Bove[71] documented a case in which a donor unit containing anti-KEL1 with a titer of 2048 was unwittingly transfused to a patient, causing immediate chills, fever of 104 F and increased pulse. In the reaction investigation, anti-KEL1 was detected in the patient's serum and in the plasma of the third unit transfused. Typing of the red blood cells of the second unit showed them to have been KEL:1. The patient never exhibited hemoglobinuria or jaundice, although it appeared that all KEL:1 red blood cells were removed from his circulation within 24 hours. Fraciosi et al[72] have reported a similar case of interdonor incompatibility due to anti-KEL1 with a titer of 16,000. In this case, retrospective typing of the donor red blood cells revealed that two out of five units transfused were KEL:1. The patient required dialysis treatment to restore urinary output.

In a classic review of hemolytic transfusion reactions occurring in a 10-year period at the Mayo Clinic, Pineda et al[73] reported 10 out of 47 reactions to be caused by anti-KEL1. One of the reactions reported was due to interdonor incompatibility. Eight cases were immediate reactions, while two were delayed reactions. Six cases documented anemia. Five patients experienced oliguria; three patients became anuric. Three patients suffered from bleeding, and death resulted in four of the cases. Again, the clinical significance of anti-KEL1 cannot be questioned.

Anti-KEL5 (-Ku) has also been shown to cause significant red blood cell destruction, often resulting in renal failure,[61,74] and Taddie et al[75] reported a case in which anti-KEL6 (-Js[a]) was implicated in a hemolytic transfusion reaction mimicking autoimmune hemolytic anemia. In this case, primary immunization to the KEL6 antigen was suggested, since no antibody had been detected in pretransfusion testing 23 days earlier.

Beattie et al[76] reported the third example of anti-KEL12 and indicated that although the patient's DAT became weakly positive after the transfusion of three KEL:12 units, the clinical response to transfusion was good; the patient's hemoglobin rose from 49 to 85 g/L (4.9 to 8.5 g/dL) within 36 hours. The antibody demonstrated a pretransfusion titer of 16, but was undetectable 3 days posttransfusion. Twenty-four hours later, the antibody titer had risen to 64.

Anti-KEL18 has been reported to cause decreased red blood cell survival. Chromium survival studies were performed on a patient with anti-KEL18 transfused with KEL:18 red blood cells. At 75 minutes, 76.6% survival was seen with only 30.7% survival noted at 24 hours. A two component destruction curve was apparent; the initial one-half disappearance time was 3.5 hours, while the second phase showed a half-time of 22.5 hours. The antibody was found to be primarily IgG4 with a small amount of IgG1 present. The subclass and a mononuclear phagocyte assay of 16% suggested that the antibody should be relatively benign, but the chromium survival study contradicted these findings by showing that accelerated red blood cell destruction did occur.[77]

Marsh et al[78] reported an example of anti-KEL19 that caused a delayed hemolytic transfusion reaction. Sharp et al[79] described a case in which a 16-year-old patient whose red blood cells demonstrated the McLeod phenotype developed anti-KEL20 (Km) posttransfusion. The IgG1 antibody was shown to cause total destruction of normal Kell phenotype red blood cells within 24 hours. A trial transfusion 2 months later of K_o red blood cells showed 67% survival at 24 hours. The patient was then transfused with five units of K_o red blood cells, resulting in an increase in hemoglobin from 50 to 82 g/L (5.0 to 8.2 g/dL). The patient's red blood cells demonstrated a negative DAT, and no additional alloantibodies were detected in his serum.

Information regarding the clinical significance of other Kell blood group system antibodies is not always available. Unfortunately, locating antigen-negative blood for patients with antibodies against high-incidence antigens may be difficult, if not impossible. In the ideal situation, the patient may preoperatively donate autologous red blood cells. Siblings of the patient may also be a source of antigen-negative red blood cells.

Ernst et al[80] determined that although the ABO and Lewis blood group systems are significant in renal transplantation, the Kell blood group system does not appear to affect cadaver renal graft survival. They describe a case in which a patient whose red blood cells were KEL:−1 and whose serum contained anti-KEL1 received a renal allograft from a living unrelated donor whose red blood cells were KEL:1. Prior to the transplant, the patient underwent a donor-specific transfusion protocol of three buffy coat preparations along with a regimen of azathioprine. The patient's anti-KEL1 titer was transiently increased, but then became negative. Following the transplant, the patient received prednisone and azathioprine, and the allograft began functioning immediately. Although rejection activity was noted on day 58 postoperatively, the serum did not reveal anti-KEL1. Rejection activity was reversed by a 10-day course of OKT3 therapy. The authors concluded that the Kell system does not seem to influence the outcome of renal graft survival—possibly because the KEL1 antigen is not present on renal tissue or is inaccessible.

Significance of Autoantibodies with Specificities Related to the Kell Blood Group System

Marsh et al[13] noted that only 10% of patients with autoantibodies related to the Kell blood group system undergo in vivo hemolysis. An autoanti-KEL1 reported by Viggiano et al[15] did not cause increased red blood cell destruction, but the IgG and IgM anti-KEL1-like antibody in the case reported by Garratty et al[22] appeared capable of binding C3 and causing immune hemolytic anemia. The IgG1 and IgG2 autoanti-KEL4 (-Kp^b) reported by Manny et al[17] in a patient with KEL:3,–4 [Kp(a+b–)] red blood cells did not bind complement or cause in vivo hemolysis. Laboratory values were normal, and an autologous ^{51}Cr-labeled study showed normal red blood cell survival. A patient with lymphoma described by Krikler et al[81] exhibited autoanti-KEL5 (-Ku). The DAT was 2+ due to IgG sensitization, but there was no clinical or laboratory evidence of hemolysis. The autoantibody disappeared with regression of the lymphoma following medication. An example of autoanti-KEL13 described by Marsh et al[19] was capable of binding C3 and did cause in vivo hemolysis.

Sullivan et al[82] reported a case in which a patient with malignant lymphoma had autoanti-Kx, which was strongly reactive with six examples of K_o red blood cells and nonreactive with nine examples of McLeod phenotype red blood cells. Testing of AET-treated common Kell phenotype red blood cells resulted in enhanced reactivity. The patient required transfusions to sustain her during a period of chemotherapy. Since no overt hemolysis was detected on transfusion of 30 mL of incompatible blood, it was decided to transfuse the patient with three units of red blood cells. Her hemoglobin rose from 60 to 92 g/L (6.0 to 9.2 g/dL) with an insignificant increase in bilirubin.

In conclusion, the clinical significance of autoantibodies with specificities related to the Kell blood group system cannot be easily predicted. Each case must be examined individually; laboratory results and the patient's response to trial transfusions of small volumes of incompatible red blood cells should be carefully evaluated before transfusing incompatible blood or withholding transfusion until antigen-negative donors can be located.

Serological Testing Methods

Manual Testing Methods

The clinical significance of Kell system antibodies necessitates the use of sensitive techniques for antibody detection and identification. As described earlier, "naturally occurring" forms of anti-KEL1 and some examples of anti-KEL2 react optimally in room temperature saline testing, but most Kell system antibodies are IgG immunoglobulins, which require the use of AHG reagents for detection. Although classical training would lead us to believe that IgG antibodies react optimally at 37 C, Arndt and Garratty[83] report that 94% of Kell system antibodies react equally well at 22 C as at 37 C and that 47% react as well at 10 C as at 37 C. At low temperatures, however, it appears that normal saline-suspended red blood cells show stronger reactions with Kell system antibodies than do red blood cells suspended in LISS solutions. Included in the 140 antibodies examined in this study were 32 examples of anti-KEL1 (-K), six anti-KEL2 (-k), one anti-KEL4 (-Kp^b) and one anti-KEL6 (-Js^a).

The use of 22% or 30% bovine serum albumin as an additive to bring about direct hemagglutination at 37 C has long been touted for Rh antibodies. Only if the "albumin layering" method of testing is performed are the Kell system antibodies sometimes detectable before the AHG phase. Also, polymerized albumin with a polymer content of 10-15% does appear to promote direct agglutination at 37 C of many Kell antibodies.[84,85]

Kell system antibodies generally show similar reactivity in enzyme testing as in routine 37 C AHG testing. Papain, ficin, bromelin and pure trypsin do not appear to affect the antigens; however, crude preparations of trypsin have been shown to weaken or destroy the KEL1 antigen.[86] Sequential treatment of red blood cells with trypsin and chymotrypsin in either order has also been shown to inactivate the KEL1 antigen.[87]

The advent of LISS and LISS additives generated several early reports of decreased sensitivity for Kell blood group system antibodies for reasons not well understood. Research done by Merry et al[88] showed that fewer Kell antibodies would bind to red blood cells suspended in 0.03M LISS than to red blood cells suspended in normal saline when one drop of serum was incubated for 20 minutes at 37 C with one drop of 5% red blood cell suspension. Modification of this procedure to involve two drops of serum and two drops of a 2.5% red blood cell suspension appeared to increase the LISS sensitivity for Kell system antibodies. Voak et al[89] also recommended this increase in serum/red blood cell ratio, which maintained the final ionic strength of 0.09M. The use of two drops of AHG reagent instead of a single drop was also found beneficial.

Another report concerning the insensitivity of LISS for Kell antibodies was made by Molthan.[90] A hemolytic transfusion reaction was caused by an anti-KEL1 that was not detected in antibody screening with a LISS additive. The IgG anti-KEL1 was later found detectable in saline or albumin at room temperature, 37 C and AHG. This case spurred a further investigation of 22 Kell system antibodies. Seven (32%) reacted weaker in tests with LISS additive than with polymerized albumin 37 C AHG testing. Three antibodies were not detected at all with the LISS additive. Tests with 2-ME showed that one of these antibodies was totally IgG, while another was only 27% IgG.[91]

The limitations of LISS in detecting Kell system antibodies became even more apparent in tests incorporating Polybrene® (hexadimethrine bromide) with a LISS potentiator. The LIP test, a LISS-Polybrene® system, allows the first state of hemagglutination to occur in a low ionic strength medium incubated at room temperature for one minute. Polybrene® is then added to cause nonspecific aggregation, bringing the antibody-sensitized red blood cells into close enough proximity to allow for crosslinking and lattice formation. The addition of a hypertonic sodium citrate-glucose solution reverses the aggregation, and agglutinates remain only when antigen-antibody complexes have been formed. Although most antibody specificities are detectable at this stage of testing, a significant number of Kell antibodies are not detectable unless the tests are washed and carried through to the AHG phase, a procedure that will be referred to as LIP-AHG.[92] Fisher[93] reported the LIP test to miss six out of 20 examples of anti-KEL1 unless the LIP-AHG tests were performed. Ferrer et al[94] examined nine examples of anti-KEL1 detected by LIP-AHG or LISS-AHG. Four antibodies were seen with LISS, but not Polybrene.® Antibody strength was not the sole factor determining reactivity, since some of the missed antibodies were very weak, while some were 2-3+. At the conclusion of this study, the hospital performing this investigation considered the lack of sensitivity for Kell antibodies significant and reverted from the LIP-AHG procedure back to their original LISS-AHG procedure.

Steane et al[95] recommended using LISS-AHG and ficin 37 C procedures for antibody screening of patients, but advocated the quicker LIP procedure for crossmatching. Out of 16 anti-KEL1 tested, 14 were detected by LIP and one by LIP-AHG. One was not detectable by either method. Out of three anti-KEL2 (-k) antibodies examined, one reacted by LIP and two required LIP-AHG testing for detection. One of two anti-KEL3 (-Kp^a) reacted by LIP, while one required LIP-AHG testing. Two examples of anti-KEL4 (-KP^b) were detectable by LIP, but one example of anti-KEL6 (-Js^a) required LIP-AHG testing for detection. The authors concluded that five of the 24 Kell system antibodies required LIP-AHG testing for detection, while one antibody was not detectable by LIP or LIP-AHG. They also noted that all 18 antibodies seen with LIP reacted weaker than with LISS-AHG procedures. Hence, their recommendations to use the more sensitive LISS-AHG procedure for antibody detection.

Mintz et al[96] compared a commercial LIP-AHG product with saline and albumin AHG testing. The kit detected 153 out of 157 antibodies; all four antibodies not detected were anti-KEL1. These four antibodies comprised 20% of the anti-KEL1 antibodies tested.

Another evaluation of the commercial LIP-AHG procedure as compared to the LISS-AHG technique was reported by Letendre et al.[97] They tested 100 coded antibodies, including 47 anti-KEL1 and three anti-KEL3, and reported that the LIP procedure failed to detect 36 antibodies [31 anti-KEL1, two anti-KEL2, two anti-FY1 (-Fy^a), and one anti-JK1 (-Jk^a)]. When converted to AHG, seven anti-KEL1 were still missed. All antibodies except two enzyme-reactive anti-RH3 (-E) were detected in LISS-AHG testing. There did not appear to be a correlation between reactivity in LISS 37 C and reactivity in LIP, nor was the antibody titer a reliable predictor of the reactivity of Kell antibodies in LIP-AHG testing. Fifty-four percent of Kell system antibodies displayed significantly higher titers in LISS testing. The authors concluded that the poor sensitivity of the Polybrene® kit for Kell system antibodies precluded its use as the primary method for antibody detection.

A newly described potentiating medium, polyethylene glycol (PEG), may offer greater hope to serologists concerned about the detection and identification of Kell system antibodies. PEG is a water soluble, industrial lubricant that contains between 68 and 84 monomeric units of PEG. It is thought to enhance antigen-antibody reactions as a result of decreased steric hindrance and/or by molecular bridging between adjacent red blood cells. A working solution of 20% weight/volume PEG in phosphate-buffered saline (PBS) is stable at 4 C. Two drops of patient serum, one drop of a 4% red blood cell suspension, and four drops of PEG solution are incubated for 15 minutes at 37 C before the red blood cells are washed and tested with anti-IgG AHG reagent. It is important to omit the customary 37 C centrifugation and reading. Nance and Garratty[98] tested one example of a strong anti-KEL1. Titration scores of 44, 36 and 52 were seen with LISS, Polybrene® and PEG, respectively. In tests with other antibody specificities, these investigators reported 64% of 25 antibodies to react stronger in PEG than in Polybrene® or LISS, 28% to react equally and 8% (2 out of 25) to react weaker. No antibody specificities went undetected in PEG testing. With PEG, Wenz et al[99] detected all 18 examples of anti-KEL1 tested, as well as three examples each of anti-KEL3 and anti-KEL6. Additional studies are necessary, but PEG with its low cost, low toxicity, stability, sensitivity, and simple procedure offers great promise for antibody detection and identification procedures.

Automated Testing Systems

Donor centers utilizing automated testing methods have also used various antibody detection methods in their attempts to detect Kell system antibodies in donor plasma. In 1971, Perrault et al[100] compared the bromelin-methylcellulose (BMC) method of Marsh with the low ionic strength Polybrene® (LISP) method of Lalezari. In testing various commercial antisera, the investigators found that anti-KEL1 antibodies were weaker with the BMC method than with manual methods. They also noted that low titer anti-KEL1 antibodies might be missed with automated testing. Confida et al[101] performed a study using the Groupamatic (Kontron Instruments, Everett, MA) and a trypsin-Polybrene®-citrate (TPC) modification of Lalezari's method, which allowed for Duffy and Kidd screening and gave more reliable results for Rh and Kell screening than did the BMC method. Still, two out of 15 examples of anti-KEL1 were not detected. These antibodies reportedly were low titered; however, five out of six high-titered examples of anti-KEL3 were not detected by TPC automated screening. The investigators concluded that the automated screening procedure was acceptable for donor screening, but was definitely unacceptable for patient screening.

In a case study reported by West et al[102] a Technicon Autogrouper Model 16 (Technicon Instruments Corporation, Tarrytown, NY) using the BMC technique for antibody screening did not detect anti-KEL1 in the plasma of a donor on five separate donations. A unit of whole blood from this donor was transfused to a patient whose red blood cells were phenotypically KEL:-1 and who had received one unit of KEL:1 blood 4 weeks before. A hemolytic transfusion reaction ensued, and the donor antibody became apparent in a minor crossmatch performed as part of the transfusion reaction investigation. Further testing revealed the titer of the donor's anti-KEL1 to be 512, and the posttransfusion patient titer to be 16. Again, the strength of the antibody did not ensure antibody detection by the automated BMC testing procedure.

Reagents That Inactivate Kell Blood Group System Antigens

The integrity of Kell system antigens is dependent on disulfide bonding between cysteine amino acid residues. Concentrations of 200-280 mM of 2-ME, β-mercaptoethylamine or dithiothrietol (DTT) (pH 8.0) have been shown to denature KEL1 (K), KEL2 (k), KEL3 (Kp^a), KEL4 (Kp^b), KEL5 (Ku), KEL6 (Js^a), KEL7 (Js^b) and YT1 (Yt^a). A solution of 1-2 mM DTT denatured only the KEL6 and KEL7 antigens, suggesting that these antigens may be different biochemically or sterically from the other Kell system antigens.[103] Later studies demonstrated that LW and YT2 (Yt^b) antigens are also destroyed by treatment of the red blood cells with DTT.[104,105] The following blood group antigens were tested and found to be unaffected by treatment with 200 mM DTT: ABO1 (A), ABO2 (B), ABO4 (A$_1$), H1 (H), I1 (I), I2 (i), RH1 (D), RH2 (C), RH3 (E), RH4 (c), RH5 (e), RH8 (C^W), LE1 (Le^a), LE2 (Le^b), FY2 (Fy^b), JK2 (Jk^b), MNS1 (M), MNS2 (N), MNS4 (s), MNS5 (U), P$_1$, PP$_1$P^k, LU1 (Lu^a), LU2 (Lu^b), MNS7 (Mi^a), MNS9 (V^W), Pr, XG1 (Xg^a), GY1 (Gy^a), Jr^a, DI2 (Di^b), Ch and Vel. This same concentration of DTT appeared to give variable results with the Gerbich antigens.[103]

In 1982, Branch and Petz[106] described a new reagent they named "Z-ZAP" or "ZZAP" that appeared to dissociate IgG molecules from the red blood cell surface. The reagent also partially denatures the MNS4 (s) and YT1 (Yt^a) antigens and totally denatures KEL1 through KEL7, KEL11 through KEL14, KEL18, KEL19, FY1 (Fy^a), FY2 (Fy^b), MNS1 (M), MNS2 (N), MNS3 (S) and the Gerbich antigens. (Antibodies directed against other Kell system antigens were not available for testing to determine whether or not additional Kell system antigens were affected by ZZAP treatment.) The following antigens were unaffected by treatment of the red blood cells with ZZAP reagent: ABO1 through 4 (A, B, AB, A$_1$), H1 (H), LE1 (Le^a), LE2 (Le^b), RH1 through RH5 (D, C, E, c, e), JK1 (Jk^a), JK2 (Jk^b), JK3, LU1 (Lu^a), LU2 (Lu^b), LU17, MNS5 (U), Vel, Lan, Jr^a, CO1 (Co^a), PP$_1$P^k, DI2 (Di^b), GY1 (Gy^a) and XK1 (Kx).

The original name of the reagent, S-SAP, described the reduction of the disulfide bonds and the activated papain component of the reagent. For "euphemistic reasons," the name was changed to Z-ZAP. This reagent consists of DTT and a proteolytic enzyme. Refer to Appendix 2-1 for the procedure. Although neither DTT nor the proteolytic enzyme will work by itself, the combination of these two chemicals will dissociate IgG molecules from the red blood cell surface. ZZAP-treated red blood cells with unbound antigen sites can then be used in warm autoadsorption procedures. The authors also suggested that ZZAP-treated red blood cells could be used for accurate Rh or Kidd typings. One must evaluate such typings with caution since commercial antisera are not licensed for use with enzyme-treated red blood cells.

Advani et al[107] reported inactivation of all Kell blood group antigens by a 6% solution of 2-AET. This reagent was shown to inactivate the following antigens: KEL1 through KEL7, KEL10 through KEL14, KEL17 through KEL22. As with the ZZAP reagent, the Kx antigen was not denatured, but was actually enhanced by AET treatment. The following antigens were not affected by treatment of the red blood cells with AET: ABO1 (A), ABO2 (B), ABO4 (A$_1$), H1 (H), I1 (I), I2 (i), LE1 (Le^a), LE2 (Le^b), Sd^a, Sd^x, Sp$_1$ (Pr), MNS1 (M), MNS2(N), MNS3(S), MNS4 (s), MNS5 (U), P$_1$, PP$_1$P^k, RH1 through RH5 (D, C, E, c, e), RH8 (C^W), RH29, LU1 (Lu^a), LU2 (Lu^b), LU3 (Lu^{ab}), FY1 (Fy^a), FY2 (Fy^b), FY3, JK1 (Jk^a), JK2 (Jk^b), JK3, XG1 (Xg^a), CO1 (Co^a), CO2 (Co^b), MNS28 (En^a), Wr^a, Wr^b, DI1 (Di^a), DI2 (Di^b), At^a, COST1 (Cs^a), Lan, Ch, Rg and Vel. Since the original report, several other investigators have reported that AET also denatures JMH, COST3 (Yk^a), COST4 (Kn^a), COST6 (McC^a), GY1 (Gy^a), GY2 (Hy), LW5 (LW^a) and YT1 (Yt^a) antigens. The variable extent of denaturation has elicited comments from several serologists.[108-111] Later studies have shown that additional antigens of the Lutheran system, contrary to the notation above, are also denatured by AET.[112,113]

These two reagents, ZZAP and AET, allow the serologist to detect antibodies underlying Kell system antibodies. In the case of ZZAP treatment, however, not all antibody specificities can be detected since some antigens of the MNSs and Duffy systems are destroyed by the proteolytic enzyme component of the ZZAP reagent. These reagents also help in the identification of antibodies directed against either highor low-incidence antigens in the Kell blood group system. They may also aid in efforts to determine more precisely the structure of various red blood cell antigens.

Conclusion

This chapter is a review of Kell system antibody specificities, their sources of stimulation, clinical significance and serological characteristics. Although transfusion services most commonly encounter anti-KEL1, the ability to detect and identify other Kell blood group system allo- and autoantibodies is necessary. Collections of rare red blood cells and sera are necessary to pinpoint the exact specificity of an antibody; however, the use of AET and/or ZZAP reagents can offer the first clue to a Kell-related antibody specificity. It is hoped that the information in this chapter will prove of value to the serologist dealing with complex serological problems.

References

1. McDowell MA, Mann JM, Milakovic K. Kell-like antibody in a Kell positive patient (abstract). Transfusion 1978;18: 389.
2. Waheed A, Kennedy MS. Delayed hemolytic transfusion reaction caused by anti-Js^b in a Js(a+b+) patient. Transfusion 1982;22:161-2.
3. Parsons SF, Judson PA, Anstee DJ. BRIC 18: A monoclonal antibody with a specificity related to the Kell blood group system. J Immunogenet 1982;9:377-80.
4. Nichols ME, Rosenfield RE, Rubinstein P. Monoclonal anti-K14 and anti-K2. Vox Sang 1987;52;231-5.
5. Sonneborn HH, Uthemann H, Pfeffer S. Monoclonal antibody specific for human blood group k (Cellano). Biotest Bull 1983;4:328-30.
6. Marsh WL, Johnson CL, Rabin BI. Antibodies associated with the Kell blood group system. First International Workshop on Monoclonal Antibodies Against Human Red Blood Cell and Related Antigens. Rev Fr Transfus Immunohematol 1988;31:383-9.
7. Zelinski R, Kaita K, Coghlan G, Lewis M. Observations on 5 monoclonal antibody samples directed against antigens in the Kell blood group system. First International Workshop on Monoclonal Antibodies Against Human Red Blood Cell and Related Antigens. Rev Fr Transfus Immunohematol 1988;31:391-4.
8. Daniels G. Kell related antibodies. First International Workshop on Monoclonal Antibodies Against Human Red Blood Cell and Related Antigens. Rev Fr Transfus Immunohematol 1988;31:395-400.
9. Parsons SF, Judson PA, Spring FA, et al. Antibodies with specificities related to the Kell blood group system. First International Workshop on Monoclonal Antibodies

Against Human Red Blood Cell and Related Antigens.Rev Fr Transfus Immunohematol 1988;31:401-5.

10. Lubenko A, Gee S, Contreras M. Report on group 7 (Kell related) antibodies. First International Workshop on Monoclonal Antibodies Against Human Red Blood Cell and Related Antigens. Rev Fr Transfus Immunohematol 1988;31:407-10.

11. Sonneborn HH, Ernst M. Evaluation of monoclonal antibodies reacting with Kell system antigens. First International Workshop on Monoclonal Antibodies Against Human Red Blood Cell and Related Antigens. Rev Fr Transfus Immunohematol 1988;31:411-15.

12. Marsh WL. Summary report of laboratories studying monoclonal antibodies in the Kell blood group system. First International Workshop on Monoclonal Antibodies Against Human Red Blood Cell and Related Antigens. Rev Fr Transfus Immunohematol 1988;31:417-8.

13. Marsh WL, Mueller KA, Johnson CL. Use of AET-treated cells in the investigation of Kell related autoimmunity (abstract). Transfusion 1982;22:419.

14. Hare V, Wilson MJ, Wilkinson S, Issitt PD. A Kell system antibody with highly unusual characteristics (abstract). Transfusion 1981;21:613.

15. Viggiano E, Clary NL, Ballas SK. Autoanti-K antibody mimicking an alloantibody. Transfusion 1982;22:329-32.

16. Beck ML, Marsh WL, Pierce SR, et al. Auto-anti-Kp[b] associated with weakened antigenicity in the Kell blood group system: A second example. Transfusion 1979;19:197-202.

17. Manny N, Levene C, Sela R, et al. Autoimmunity and the Kell blood groups: Auto anti-Kp[b] in a Kp(a+b−) patient. Vox Sang 1983;45:252-6.

18. Puig N, Carbonell F, Marty ML. Another example of mimicking anti-Kp[b] in a Kp(a+b−) patient. Vox Sang 1986;51:57-9.

19. Marsh WL, DiNapoli J, Øyen R. Autoimmune hemolytic anemia caused by anti-K13.Vox Sang 1979;36:174-8.

20. Issitt PD. Serology and genetics of the Rhesus blood group system. Cincinnati: Montgomery Scientific Publications, 1979;167-8.

21. Marsh WL, Øyen R, Alicea E, et al. Autoimmune hemolytic anemia and the Kell blood groups. Am J Hematol 1979;7:155-62.

22. Garratty G, Sattler MS, Petz LD, Flannery EP. Immune hemolytic anemia associated with anti-Kell and a carrier

state for chronic granulomatous disease. Rev Fr Transfus Immunohematol 1979;22:529-49.

23. Issitt PD. Applied blood group serology. 3rd ed. Miami: Montgomery Scientific Publications, 1985:301.

24. Seyfried H, Górska B, Maj S, et al. Apparent depression of antigens of the Kell blood group system associated with autoimmune acquired hemolytic anemia. Vox Sang 1972;23:528-36.

25. Vengelen-Tyler V, Gonzalez B, Garratty G, et al. Acquired loss of red cell Kell antigens. Br J Hematol 1987;65:231-4.

26. Mollison PL. Blood transfusion in clinical medicine. 7th ed. Oxford: Blackwell Scientific Publications, 1983:402-7.

27. Allen FH, Warshaw AL. Blood group sensitization: A comparison of antigens K1 (Kell) and c (hr'). Vox Sang 1962;7:222-7.

28. Kornstad L, Heistø H. The frequency of formation of Kell antibodies in recipients of Kell-positive blood (abstract). Proceedings of the 6th Congress of the European Society of Hematology. Basel: Karger, 1958:754-8.

29. Giblett ER. A critique of the theoretical hazard of inter- vs. intra-racial transfusion. Transfusion 1961;1:233-8.

30. Garratty G. Factors affecting the pathogenicity of red cell auto- and alloantibodies. In: Nance SJ, ed. Immune destruction of red blood cells. Arlington: American Association of Blood Banks, 1989:109-69.

31. Hunt JS, Beck ML, Hardman JT, et al. Characterization of human erythrocyte alloantibodies by IgG subclass and monocyte interaction. Am J Clin Pathol 1980;74:259-64.

32. Michaelsen TE, Kornstad L. IgG subclass distribution of anti-Rh, anti-Kell and anti-Duffy antibodies measured by sensitive haemagglutination assays. Clin Exp Immunol 1987;67:637-45.

33. Hardman JT, Beck ML. Haemagglutination in capillaries: correlation with blood group specificity and IgG subclass. Transfusion 1981;21:343-6.

34. Hopkins DF. Saline agglutinating anti-K and anti-k in the apparent absence of IgM antibody. Br J Haematol 1970; 19:749-53.

35. Morgan P, Bossom EL. "Naturally-occurring" anti-Kell (K1): two examples. Transfusion 1963;3:397-8.

36. Mukumoto Y, Konishi H, Ito K, et al. An example of naturally occurring anti-Kell (K1) in a Japanese male. Vox Sang 1978;35:275-6.

37. Tegoli J, Sausais L, Issitt PD. Another example of a naturally-occurring anti-K1. Vox Sang 1967;12:305-7.
38. Marsh WL, Nichols ME, Øyen R, et al. Naturally occurring anti-Kell stimulated by *E. coli* enterocolitis in a 20-day old child. Transfusion 1978;18:149-54.
39. Kanel GC, Davis I, Bowman JE. "Naturally-occurring" anti-K1: Possible association with mycobacterium infection. Transfusion 1978;18:472-3.
40. McGinniss MH, MacLowry JD, Holland PV. Acquisition of K:1-like antigen during terminal sepsis. Transfusion 1984;24:28-30.
41. Pereira A, Monteagudo J, Rovira M, et al. Anti-K1 of the IgA class associated with *Morganella morganii* infection. Transfusion 1989;29:549-51.
42. O'Brien M, King G, Dube VE, et al. Anti-Kell (K1) in idiopathic thrombocytopenic purpura. Transfusion 1979;19:558-61.
43. Judd WJ, Walter WJ, Steiner EA. Clinical and laboratory findings on two patients with naturally occurring anti-Kell agglutinins. Transfusion 1981;21:184-8.
44. Savalónis JM, Kalish RI, Cummings EA, Ryan RW, Aloisi R. Kell blood group activity of gram-negative bacteria. Transfusion 1988;28:229-32.
45. Schmidt PJ, McGinniss MH, Leyshon WC, Kevy SV. An anti-k (anti-Cellano) serum with the properties of a complete saline agglutinin. Vox Sang 1958;3:438-41.
46. Thomas MJ, Konugres AA. An anti-K2 (Cellano) serum with unusual properties.Vox Sang 1966;11:227-9.
47. Dinning G, Doughty RW, Collins AK. A further example of IgM anti-K2 (Cellano). Vox Sang 1985;48:317-8.
48. Ito K, Mukumoto Y, Konishi H. An example of "naturally-occurring" anti-Js[a] (K6) in a Japanese female. Vox Sang 1979;37:350-1.
49. Race RR, Sanger R. Blood groups in man. Oxford: Blackwell Scientific Publications, 1975:283-305.
50. Weinstein L. Irregular antibodies causing haemolytic disease of the newborn. Obstet Gynecol Surv 1976;31:581-91.
51. Hardy J, Napier JAF. Red cell antibodies detected in antenatal tests on Rhesus positive women in south and mid-Wales. Br J Obstet Gynaecol 1981;88:91-100.
52. Pepperell RJ, Barrie JU, Fliegner JR. Significance of red-cell irregular antibodies in the obstetric patient. Med J Austral 1977;64:453-6.

53. Wenk RE, Goldstein P, Felix JK. Kell alloimmunization, hemolytic disease of the newborn, and perinatal management. Obstet Gynecol 1985;66:473-6.
54. Leventhal ML, Wolf AM. Erythroblastosis (hydrops) fetalis from Kell sensitization. Am J Obstet Gynecol 1956; 71:452-4.
55. Kanhai HH, Gravenhorst JB, Gemke RJ, et al. Fetal blood group determination in first trimester pregnancy for the management of severe immunization. Am J Obstet Gynecol 1987;156:120-3.
56. Rodesch F, Lambermont M, Donner C, et al. Chorionic biopsy in management of severe Kell alloimmunization. Am J Obstet Gynecol 1987;156:124-5.
57. Bowman JM, Harman FA, Manning CR, Pollock JM. Erythroblastosis fetalis produced by anti-k. Vox Sang 1989;56:187-9.
58. Jensen KG. Haemolytic disease of the newborn caused by anti-Kp[a]. Vox Sang 1962;7:476-8.
59. Anderson L, White JB, Liles BA, Jack JA. A case of haemolytic disease of the newborn due to anti-Kp[b] (Rautenberg). Am J Med Technol 1959;25:184-8.
60. Wright J, Cornwall SM, Matsina E. A second example of hemolytic disease of the newborn due to anti-Kp[b]. Vox Sang 1965;10:218-21.
61. Chown B, Lewis M, Kaita H. A "new" Kell blood-group phenotype. Nature 1957;180:711.
62. Donovan LM, Tripp KL, Zuckerman JE, Konugres AA. Hemolytic disease of the newborn due to anti-Js[a]. Transfusion 1973;13:153.
63. Levene C, Rudolphson Y, Shechter Y. A second case of hemolytic disease of the newborn due to anti-Js[a]. Transfusion 1980;20:714-5.
64. Wake EJ, Issitt PD, Reihart JK, et al. Hemolytic disease of the newborn due to anti-Js[b]. Transfusion 1969;9:217-8.
65. Lowe RF, Musengezi AT, Moores P. Severe hemolytic disease of the newborn associated with anti-Js[b]. Transfusion 1978;18:466-8.
66. Wallace ME, Bouysou C, DeJongh DS, et al. Anti-K:14: An antibody specificity associated with the Kell blood group system. Vox Sang 1976;30:300-4.
67. Manny N, Levene C, Harel N, et al. The second example of anti-K22 and a family genetically informative for K and K22. Vox Sang 1985;49:135-7.

68. Bar Shany S, Ben Porath DB, Levene C, et al. K22, a "new" para-Kell antigen of high frequency. Vox Sang 1982;42:87-90.

69. Marsh WL, Redman CM, Kessler LA, et al. K23. A low incidence antigen in the Kell blood group system identified by biochemical characterization. Transfusion 1987;27:36-40.

70. Ottensooser F, Mellone O, Biancalana A. Fatal transfusion reaction due to the Kell factor. Blood 1953;8:1029-33.

71. Zettner A, Bove JR. Hemolytic transfusion reaction due to interdonor incompatibility. Transfusion 1963;3:48-51.

72. Fraciosi RA, Awer E, Santana M. Interdonor incompatibility resulting in anuria. Transfusion 1967;7:297-8.

73. Pineda AA, Brzica SM, Taswell HF. Hemolytic transfusion reaction. Recent experience in a large blood bank. Mayo Clin Proc 1978;53:378-90.

74. Nunn HD, Giles CM, Dormandy KM. A second example of anti-Ku in a patient who has the rare Kell phenotype K_o. Vox Sang 1965;11:611-19.

75. Taddie SJ, Barrasso C, Ness PM. A delayed transfusion reaction caused by anti-K6. Transfusion 1982;22:68-9.

76. Beattie KM, Heinz B, Korol S, et al. Third example of anti-K12: Successful transfusion with K:12 blood (abstract). Transfusion 1978;18:383-4.

77. Barrasso C, Baldwin ML, Drew H, Ness PM. In vivo survival of K:18 red cells in a recipient with anti-K18. Transfusion 1983;23:258-9.

78. Marsh WL, DiNapoli J, Øyen R, et al. Delayed hemolytic transfusion reaction caused by the second example of anti-K19. Transfusion 1979;19:604-8.

79. Sharp D, Rogers S, Dickstein B, et al. Successful transfusion of K_o blood to a Km-Kx- patient with anti-Km (abstract). Transfusion 1988;28(Suppl);37S.

80. Ernst RL, Meredith WT, Blackmore MA, Shield CF. The Kell system and kidney transplantation. Transplantation 1987;43:759-61.

81. Krikler SH, Turner-Lienaux K, Godin T, Miller W. Auto-anti-K5 (Ku) in a patient with lymphoma (letter). Vox Sang 1987;52:157.

82. Sullivan CM, Kline WE, Rabin BI, et al. The first example of autoanti-Kx. Transfusion 1987;27:322-4.

83. Arndt P, Garratty G. Evaluation of the optimal incubation temperature for detecting certain IgG antibodies with

potential clinical significance. Transfusion 1988;28:210-13.

84. Reckel RP, Harris J. The unique characteristics of co-valently polymerized bovine albumin solutions when used as antibody detection media. Transfusion 1978; 18:397-406.

85. Fitzsimmons J, Morel P. The effects of red blood cell suspending media on hemagglutination and the anti-globulin test. Transfusion 1979;19:81-5.

86. Morton JA. Some observations on the action of blood group antibodies on red cells treated with proteolytic enzymes. Br J Haematol 1962;8:134-48.

87. Judson PA, Anstee DJ. Comparative effects of trypsin and chymotrypsin on blood group antigens. Med Lab Sci 1977;34:1-6.

88. Merry AH, Thomson EE, Langar J, et al. Quantitation of antibody binding to erythrocytes in LISS. Vox Sang 1984; 47:125-32.

89. Voak D, Downie M, Haigh T, Cook N. Improved antiglob-ulin tests to detect difficult antibodies: Detection of anti-Kell by LISS. Med Lab Sci 1982;39:363-70.

90. Molthan L, Strohm PL. Hemolytic transfusion reaction due to anti-Kell undetectable in low-ionic-strength solu-tions. Am J Clin Pathol 1981;75:629-31.

91. Molthan L. An evaluation of a low ionic strength saline-bovine albumin medium for human red cell antigen-an-tibody testing. Can J Med Tech 1981;43:176-9.

92. Lalezari P, Jiang AF. The manual Polybrene test: A simple and rapid procedure for detection of red cell antibodies. Transfusion 1980;20:206-11.

93. Fisher GA. Use of the manual Polybrene test in the routine hospital laboratory. Transfusion 1983;23:151-4.

94. Ferrer Z, Wright J, Moore BPL, Freedman J. Comparison of a modified manual hexadimethrine bromide (Poly-brene) and a low-ionic-strength solution antibody detec-tion technique. Transfusion 1985;25:145-8.

95. Steane EA, Steane SM, Montgomery SR, Pearson JR. A proposal for compatibility testing incorporating the man-ual hexadimethrine bromide (Polybrene) test. Transfu-sion 1985;25:540-4.

96. Mintz PD, Anderson G. Comparison of a manual hexa-dimethrine bromide-antiglobulin test with saline and albumin antiglobulin tests for pretransfusion testing. Transfusion 1987;27:134-7.

97. Letendre PL, Williams MA, Ferguson DJ. Comparison of a commercial hexadimethrine bromide method and low ionic strength solution for antibody detection with special reference to anti-K. Transfusion 1987;27:138-41.

98. Nance S, Garratty G. A new potentiator of red blood cell antigen-antibody reactions. Am J Clin Pathol 1987;5: 633-5.

99. Wenz B, Apuzzo J. Polyethylene glycol improves the indirect antiglobulin test. Transfusion 1989;29:218-20.

100. Perrault R, Hogman C. Automated red cell antibody analysis: A parallel study. Vox Sang 1971;20:340-55.

101. Confida S, Hurel C, Chesnel N, et al. Red blood cell antibody screening with Groupamatic system. Vox Sang 1981;40:34-43.

102. West NC, Jenkins JA, Johnston BR, Modi N. Interdonor incompatibility due to anti-Kell antibody undetectable by automated antibody screening. Vox Sang 1986;50:174-6.

103. Branch DR, Petz LD. Disulfide bonds are a requirement for Kell and Cartwright (Yt^a) blood group antigen integrity. Br J Haematol 1983;54:573-78.

104. Konigshaus G, Holland T. The effect of dithiothreitol on the LW antigen. Transfusion 1984;24:536-7.

105. Shulman I, Nelson J, Lam HT. Loss of Yt^b antigen activity after treatment of red cells with either dithiothreitol or 2-mercaptoethanol (letter). Transfusion 1986;26:214.

106. Branch DR, Petz LD. A new reagent (ZZAP) having multiple applications in immunohematology. Am J Clin Pathol 1982;78:161-7.

107. Advani H, Zamor J, Judd WJ, et al. Inactivation of Kell blood group antigens by 2-aminoethylisothiouronium bromide. Br J Haematol 1982;51:107-15.

108. Marsh W, Johnson C, Mueller K. AET-treated red cells (letter). Transfusion 1983;23:275.

109. Moulds J, Moulds M. Inactivation of Kell blood group antigens by 2-aminoethylisothiouronium bromide (letter). Transfusion 1983;23:274.

110. Levene C, Harel N. 2-aminoethylisothiouronium-treated red cells and the Cartwright (Yt^a) antigen (letter). Transfusion 1984;24:541.

111. Moulds J, Moulds M, Patriquin P. Inactivation of LW^a by 2-aminoethylisothiouronium bromide (letter). Transfusion 1986;26:305.

112. Levene C, Karniel Y, Sela R. 2-Aminoethylisothiouronium bromide-treated red cells and the Lutheran antigens Lu^a

and Lu^b (letter). Transfusion 1987;27:505-6.

113. Daniels G. The Lutheran blood group system: Monoclonal antibodies, biochemistry and the effect of *In(Lu)*. In: Pierce SR, Macpherson CR, eds. Blood group systems: Duffy, Kidd and Lutheran. Arlington, VA: American Association of Blood Banks, 1988:119-47.

Appendix 2-1. ZZAP Treatment of Red Blood Cells

Purpose:

ZZAP artificially creates enzyme-treated K_o red blood cells that can be used to help identify alloantibodies in sera containing an antibody directed against a high incidence antigen in the Kell blood group system. In addition, red blood cells treated with ZZAP can be helpful in determining whether or not an antibody is directed against a low or high incidence antigen in the Kell blood group system.

Principle:

The dithiothreitol (DTT) in the reagent may denature Kell system antigens by reductive cleavage of disulfide bonds between cysteine amino acid residues which maintain antigenic integrity.

Materials:

1. DTT (Cleland's reagent)
2. Enzyme
3. Phosphate-buffered saline (PBS)
4. Isotonic saline

Procedure:

Preparation of ZZAP reagent:

1. Prepare 0.2M DTT by dissolving 1 g DTT (Cleland's reagent) in 32.4 mL of 0.15 M PBS (pH 7.3). Dispense into 2.5 mL aliquots. Store at temperatures below –20 C.
2. Prepare a 1% weight/volume enzyme solution in PBS (pH 7.3). Either ficin, cysteine-activated papain or trypsin may be used. Dispense into 0.5 mL aliquots. Store at temperatures below –20 C.
3. Dispense PBS (pH 7.3) into 2 mL aliquots. Store at 4 C.
4. For a working solution of ZZAP, mix together one aliquot of each of the three above solutions. Working solution is not stable for more than 5 days when stored at 4 C, but is best when prepared immediately before use.

Treatment of red blood cells for preparation of enzyme-treated K_o red blood cells:

1. Wash 2 drops of a 3% suspension of red blood cells once in a large volume of isotonic saline.
2. Remove all saline and add 2 drops of working ZZAP solution.
3. Incubate at 37 C for 30 minutes.
4. Wash four times with large volumes of isotonic saline and resuspend to 2-3% suspension prior to testing in desired phases.

Note: As a control, a KEL:1 red blood cell sample should be ZZAP-treated and tested with anti-KEL1 to ensure that the treatment has inactivated the Kell system antigens.

Interpretation:

Reactivity with ZZAP-treated red blood cells indicates that the antibody is not defining an antigen in the Kell blood group system.

No reactivity with ZZAP-treated red blood cells, but reactivity with untreated red blood cells indicates that the antibody may be reacting with an antigen in the Kell blood group system or with other antigens denatured by ZZAP, such as FY1 (Fy^a), FY2 (Fy^b), MNS1 (M), MNS2 (N), MNS3 (S), YT1 (Yt^a) and Gerbich.

References:

1. Branch DR, Petz LD. A new reagent (ZZAP) having multiple applications in immunohematology. Am J Clin Pathol 1982; 78:161-7.
2. Judd J. Methods in Immunohematology. Miami: Montgomery Scientific Publications, 1988:49-50.

Appendix 2-2. 2-Aminoethylisothiouronium Bromide (AET) Treatment of Red Blood Cells

Purpose:

AET artificially creates K_o red blood cells that can be used to help identify alloantibodies in sera containing an antibody directed against a high incidence antigen in the Kell blood group system. In addition, red blood cells treated with AET can be helpful in determining whether or not an antibody is directed against a low or high incidence antigen in the Kell blood group system.

Principle:

AET may denature Kell system antigens by reductive cleavage of disulfide bonds between cysteine amino acid residues which maintain antigenic integrity.

Materials:

1. 6% AET (6 g/100 mL deionized water) adjusted to pH 8.0 with 5N NaOH. Note: Prepare fresh immediately before use.

2. Isotonic saline.

Procedure:

1. Wash 3 drops of a 5% suspension of red blood cells once in a large volume of isotonic saline.
2. Remove all saline and add 6 drops of 6% AET to the packed red blood cells.
3. Incubate at 37 C for 30 minutes.
4. Wash four times with large volumes of isotonic saline.
5. Add 2 drops of serum to each tube of treated red blood cells and carry out testing in desired phases.
6. Use anti-IgG reagents when performing AHG tests with AET-treated red blood cells because these red blood cells nonspecifically bind complement.

Note: As a control, a KEL:1 red blood cell sample should be AET-treated and tested with anti-KEL1 to ensure that the treatment has inactivated the Kell system antigens.

Interpretation:

Reactivity with AET-treated red blood cells with no reduction in strength as compared to that seen with untreated red blood cells indicates that the antibody is not defining an antigen in the Kell blood group system.

No reactivity with AET-treated red blood cells, but reactivity with untreated red blood cells indicates that the antibody may be reacting with an antigen in the Kell blood group system. Other antigens which may be denatured by AET treatment include JMH, COST 3 (Yk^a), COST 4 (Kn^a), COST 6 (McC^a), GY2 (Hy), YT1 (Yt^a), and Lutheran antigens.

References:

1. Advani H, Zamor J, Judd WJ, Johnson, CL, Marsh WL. Inactivation of Kell blood group system antigens by 2-aminoethyl-isothiouronium bromide. Br J Haematol 1982; 51:107-15.
2. Moulds J, Moulds M. Inactivation of Kell blood group antigens by 2-aminoethylisothiouronium bromide (letter). Transfusion 1983;23:274.
3. Levene C, Harel N. 2-aminoethylisothiouronium-treated red cells and the Cartwright (Yt^a) antigen (letter). Transfusion 1984; 24:541.

In: Laird-Fryer B, Daniels G and Levitt J, eds.
Blood Group Systems: Kell
Arlington, VA: American Association
of Blood Banks, 1990

3

Biochemistry of the Kell Blood Group

Joan C. Pehta, MD, Colvin M. Redman, PhD, and
W. Laurence Marsh, PhD, FRCPath, FIBiol, FIMLS

C OMPREHENSIVE UNDERSTANDING OF A red cell blood group requires knowledge from several perspectives. From the clinical viewpoint it is necessary to define its importance in transfusion medicine. Understanding at the basic science level requires information concerning any phenotypic complexity, and the formal genetics and molecular biology of the background from which it arises. The biochemist must define the nature of the immunodeterminants and the red blood cell membrane component that carries them, while related studies establish the biological function of the particular membrane structure. These are challenges for blood group research in the next decade, for in no major blood group is this depth of information available.

Blood group antigenicity may be a characteristic of a red blood cell surface exposed membrane protein or the carbohydrate moiety of a glycoprotein or glycolipid. Biochemical characterization requires isolation of a red blood cell antigenic structure as the first stage in the investigation. When antigen specificity is determined by the nature of an immunodominant sugar, characterization is more straightforward for the sugar

Joan C. Pehta, MD, Associate Immunohematologist, The New York Blood Center; Colvin M. Redman, PhD, Senior Investigator, Laboratory of Membrane Biochemistry, The Lindsley F. Kimball Research Institute of The New York Blood Center; W. Laurence Marsh, PhD, FRCPath, FIBiol, FIMLS, Senior Vice President for Research, The Lindsley F. Kimball Research Institute of The New York Blood Center, New York, New York.
Supported by a grant from the National Institutes of Health

(and the antigen) usually survives the rigors of the isolation process. When antigen activity is determined by the nature of a protein or glycoprotein, characterization is often more diffi- cult. In these cases it appears that the in situ arrangement of the protein molecule and its conformation on the red blood cell are important factors in maintaining the proper surface topog- raphy, which confers recognizable antigen activity. The milieu in the lipid bilayer of the red blood cell membrane also plays an important role in maintaining protein molecules in their proper relationship, as evidenced by the observation that treat- ment of red blood cell membranes with phospholipase A2 inactivates antigens of the Rh[1] and Kell blood group systems. Several of the blood group proteins lose their ability to react with blood group antibodies when red blood cell membranes are dissolved in detergents or other solvents. Rh and Kell antibodies, for example, give no reaction when they are used as probes in Western immunoblot experiments against solubi- lized red blood cell membrane proteins. However, one report has described isolation of a KEL1 antigen protein that inhibited anti-KEL1 in serological tests.[2]

Isolation of Kell Antigen Protein

Early studies showed that red blood cell Kell antigens are inactivated by heating red blood cells at 56 C, by inactivation in a crude trypsin solution, by reduction with sulfhydryl com- pounds or by incubating red blood cells in formaldehyde solu- tion.[3-5] These procedures denature proteins. Other studies identified a KEL1-like antigen on a coliform organism and established that carbohydrate was a factor in its KEL1-like activity.[3] These data indicated that Kell antigens were markers on a red blood cell membrane glycoprotein, but whether the carbohydrate or the protein moiety determined specificity was unknown. First attempts to isolate Kell antigen structures by passage of solubilized red blood cell membranes through affin- ity columns loaded with potent anti-KEL7 were unsuccessful. In retrospect the failure was probably caused by loss of Kell antigen integrity when the red blood cell membranes were solubilized.

Isolation of Kell antigen protein was achieved by application of the method first used by Moore et al[6] to isolate red blood cell membrane proteins associated with the RH1 (D), RH3 (E), RH4 (c), and FY1 (Fy^a) antigens. In this procedure the antigen on intact red blood cells is complexed with an appropriate IgG blood group antibody and, following detergent solubilization of the membrane, immune complexes are isolated with Protein A-Sepharose or an antibody to IgG attached to Sepharose. Sensitivity of protein detection is increased if surface-exposed red blood cell membrane proteins are first radiolabeled by lactoperoxidase catalyzed iodination. Analysis of immune complexes eluted from the Protein A-Sepharose, using sodium dodecylsulfate polyacrylamide gel electrophoresis (SDS-PAGE) under reducing conditions yields the heavy and light chains of the IgG Kell antibody and a 93-kDa radiolabeled protein that carries the Kell group antigens.[7] Figure 3-1 is a composite of the isolation and analysis by SDS-PAGE of Kell protein and is representative of many studies. When the isolated immune complexes are analyzed by SDS-PAGE under nonreducing conditions Kell protein migrates at approximately 85 kDa. The finding that Kell protein has greater electrophoretic mobility under nonreducing conditions indicates that the 85-kDa protein has intra chain disulfide bonds that retain it in a folded configuration.[8] Using this procedure of immunoprecipitation, Kell antigen protein has been isolated with anti-KEL1, -KEL2, -KEL4, -KEL5, -KEL7, -KEL12, -KEL14, -KEL18, -KEL19, -KEL22, -KEL23 and with IgG autoantibody having serologic specificity in the Kell system. In each case a 93-kDa protein was recovered. The isolated protein stains by the periodic acid Schiff technique, establishing that it is a glycoprotein. Treatment of the glycoprotein with N-glyconase, an enzyme that removes N-linked sugars, reduces the molecular mass to 78-80 kDa. If an average size of 2500 daltons is assumed for an oligosaccharide side chain, Kell protein probably carries five to six N-linked oligosaccharide side chains on the surface exposed portion of the molecule. Biochemical studies have established that different Kell antibodies isolate almost identical proteins. It appears that the various Kell antigens are markers on a single species of red blood cell membrane glycoprotein.

Independence of the Kell Glycoprotein From Band 3 Protein

Kell and band 3 glycoproteins migrate by SDS-PAGE with similar molecular mass. It was important, therefore, to determine whether Kell is a component of band 3, the anion transport protein. Several studies show that they are different proteins. Analysis and comparison of two-dimensional tryptic and chymotryptic peptide maps of the two proteins show marked differences, and the two proteins have different amino acid compositions. A rabbit polyclonal antibody against Kell

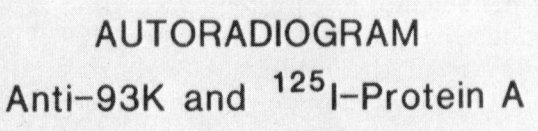

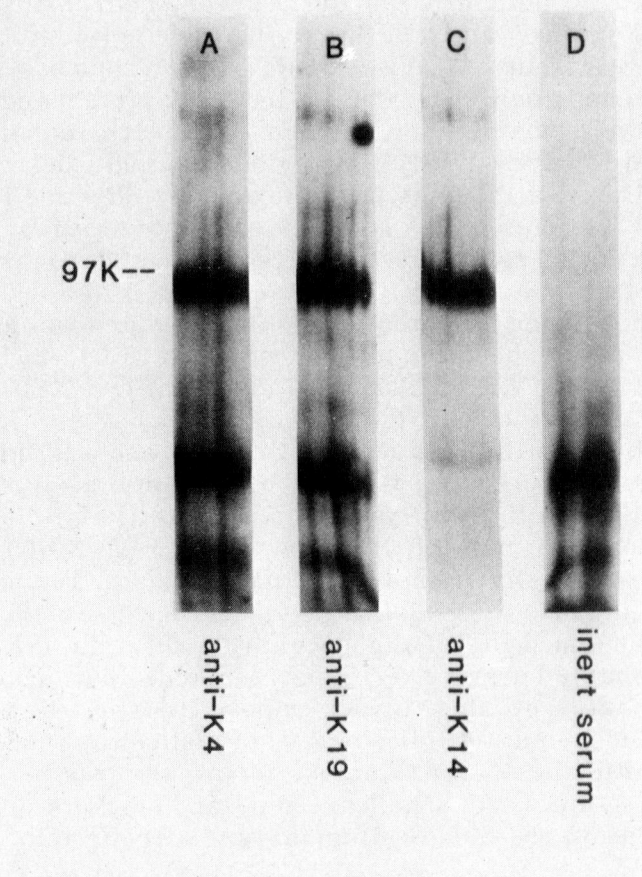

Figure 3-1. Western blot of Kell (93-kDa) protein immunoprecipitated from common Kell phenotype red blood cells. Red blood cells were incubated with various Kell antibodies, lysed and detergent solubilized. Immune complexes were recovered with protein A-Sepharose. After SDS-PAGE under reducing conditions the separated proteins were transferred by Western blot, probed with rabbit anti-Kell and visualized by autoradiography with ^{125}I-protein A. Common Kell phenotype red blood cells (A) treated with anti-KEL4, (B) treated with anti-KEL19 , (C) treated with anti-KEL14 and (D) inert serum control.

protein does not react with band 3 protein, and an antibody to band 3 does not react with isolated Kell protein. Other biochemical studies also show differences that Kell and band 3 are different membrane glycoproteins with similar mass.[8]

Interaction of Kell Protein With the Red Blood Cell Cytoskeleton

Isolation of Kell protein under nonreducing conditions yields a series of protein complexes with molecular sizes from 85 kDa up to more than 200 kDa. Each complex contains Kell protein together with other proteins that are not labeled by surface iodination. Analysis of these proteins shows that they are components of the red blood cell cytoskeleton—namely, spectrin, actin and band 4.1. These data indicate that Kell is a transmembrane glycoprotein with the cytoplasmic portion of the molecule complexed with the red blood cell cytoskeleton.[8,9]

Biochemistry of K_o and McLeod Red Blood Cells

K_o (Kell$_{null}$) red blood cells lack all known antigens that are products of the *KEL* gene. The cells are KEL:–1,–2,–3,–4 etc. Immunoprecipitation experiments with K_o red blood cells using potent human polyclonal, and murine monoclonal, Kell antibodies yield no evidence of the Kell 93-kDa protein. In addition a rabbit polyclonal antibody, produced by injection of isolated reduced Kell protein, does not react with K_o red blood cell membranes when tested by Western immunoblot technique. It appears that K_o red blood cells lack both Kell group antigens and the carrier protein that bears them.[8]

McLeod red blood cells have a common Kell phenotype but with extraordinarily weak Kell antigens.[10] Immunoprecipitation studies using McLeod red blood cells and Kell antibodies yield the 93-kDa Kell protein but in greatly reduced amount.[11] In addition, McLeod red blood cell membrane proteins separated by SDS-PAGE and transferred to nitrocellulose paper, react weakly by Western immunoblotting with the rabbit polyclonal antibody to Kell protein, giving a reaction band at 93 kDa.[11] These data establish that, from the biochemical perspective, Kell antigens on McLeod red blood cells are not occluded in the red blood cell membrane and are not attached to a different carrier. The difference between the Kell proteins in red blood cells of common Kell and McLeod types appears to be mainly quantitative.

Isolation of Kx Antigen

Kx antigen has an almost ubiquitous distribution on red blood cells but is absent from McLeod red blood cells. K_o red blood cells lack antigens of the Kell complex and have enhanced Kx activity. Immunoprecipitation experiments with red blood cells of common Kell type using anti-Kx yield a protein that migrates by SDS-PAGE with a molecular mass of 37 kDa.[11] Figure 3-2 shows SDS-PAGE analysis of Kx protein under reducing conditions. Similar studies using K_o red blood cells yield about twice the amount of the 37-kDa Kx protein, but studies with McLeod red blood cells yield none at all. Quantitative experiments, in which Kx protein was radioiodinated before isolation, show that Kx positive red blood cells have only a small amount of Kx protein. Only 0.0076-0.014% of ^{125}I-labeled cell-surface proteins is separated from K_o red blood cells when treated with anti-Kx compared with 0.07-0.1% that is isolated from Kell-positive red blood cells when treated with Kell antibodies.[11] This small amount of Kx protein makes it unlikely that it has a significant structural role in the red blood cell membrane but probably acts through a catalytic function.

The Nature of Kell Immunodeterminants

The biochemical basis for intragroup specificity in the Kell system is still unknown. Some years ago, before biochemical information was available, a model was suggested for the Kell blood group system in which specificities were determined by immunodominant sugars attached to a polypeptide backbone that carried the Kx marker. The Kell system would, thus, consist of a series of closely linked genes controlling transferase enzymes.[12] The biochemical data show that Kell and Kx are markers on different proteins and that Kx protein, on normal red blood cells, is not an integral component of Kell protein. The early hypothetical pathway is not supported by biochemical data. It is now considered more likely that Kell antigen differences are a reflection of variation in the exposed protein moiety of the Kell glycoprotein. Carbohydrate may be involved in formation of the immunodeterminants but it is unlikely that it is the major determining factor in specificity.

Editors' Comment: For a more detailed description of Kell blood group system biochemical analysis, consult this chapter's references 7, 8 and 11, as well as the following references: Marsh WL, Redman CM. Recent development in the Kell blood

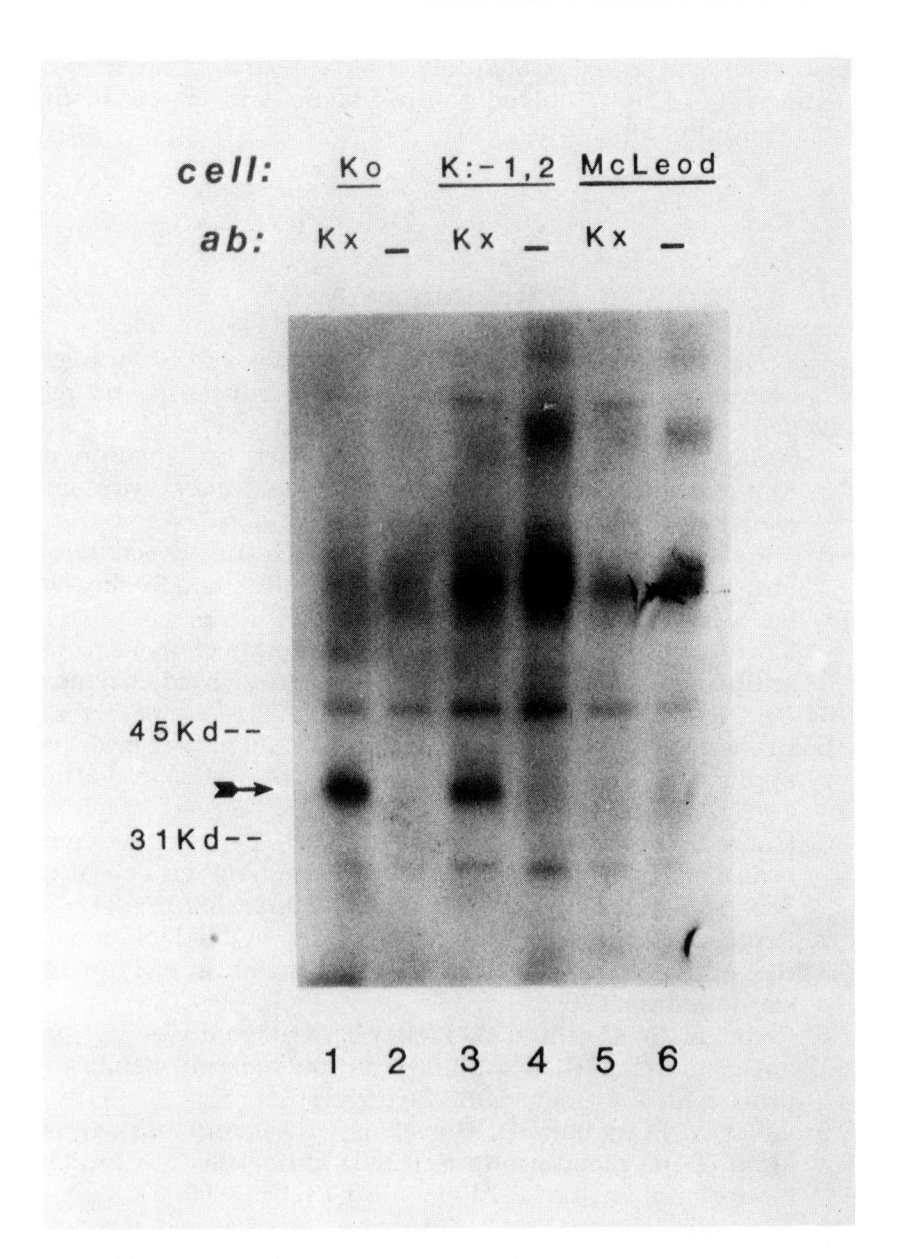

Figure 3-2. Results with SDS-PAGE on 7.5% polyacrylamide gels under reducing condition for separation of Kx (37-kDa) protein from red blood cells of various Kell phenotypes. Red blood cells were surface-labeled with ^{125}I, incubated with antibody against Kx, lysed and detergent-solubilized. Immune complexes were recovered with protein A-Sepharose. After elution, the immunoprecipitated proteins were visualized by autoradiography. Lane (1) K_o red blood cells treated with anti-Kx, (2) K_o red blood cells treated with nonimmune serum, (3) common Kell phenotype red blood cells treated with anti-Kx, (4) common Kell phenotype red blood cells treated with nonimmune serum, (5) McLeod red blood cells treated with anti-Kx and (6) McLeod red blood cells treated with nonimmune serum.

group system. Transfus Med Rev 1987;1:4-20 and Marsh WL, Redmen CM. The Kell blood group system: A review. Transfusion 1990;30:158-67.

References

1. Hughes-Jones NC, Green EJ, Hunt V. Loss of Rh antigen activity following the action of phospholipase A2 on red cell stroma. Vox Sang 1975;29:184-91.
2. Wallas C, Simon R, Sharpe MA, Byler C. Isolation of Kell-reactive protein from red cell membranes. Transfusion 1986;26:173-6.
3. Marsh WL, Nichols ME, Øyen R, et al. Naturally occurring anti-Kell stimulated by *E. coli* Enterocolitis in a 20 day old child. Transfusion 1978;18:149-54.
4. Morton JA. Some observations on the action of blood group antibodies on red cells treated with proteolytic enzymes. Br J Haematol 1962;8:134-48.
5. Branch DR, Petz LD. A new reagent (ZZAP) having multiple applications in immunohematology. Am J Clin Pathol 1982;78:161.
6. Moore S, Woodrow CF, McClelland DBL. Isolation of membrane components associated with human red cell antigens Rh(D), (c), (E) and Fy^a. Nature 1982;259:529-31.
7. Redman CM, Marsh WL, Mueller KA, et al. Isolation of Kell-active protein from the red cell membrane. Transfusion 1984;24:176-8.
8. Redman CM, Avellino G, Pfeffer S et al. Kell blood group antigens are part of a 93,000 dalton red cell membrane protein. J Biol Chem 1986;261:9521-5.
9. Jaber A, Blanchard D, Goossens CB, et al. Characterization of the blood group Kell (K1) antigen with a human monoclonal antibody. Blood 1989;73:1597-1602.
10. Allen FH, Krabbe SMR, Corcoran PA. A new phenotype (McLeod) in the Kell blood group system. Vox Sang 1961; 6:555-60.
11. Redman CM, Marsh WL, Scarborough A, et al. Biochemical studies on McLeod phenotype red cells and isolation of Kx antigens. Br J Haematol 1988;68:131-6.
12. Marsh WL, Øyen R, Nichols ME, Allen FH. Chronic granulomatous disease and the Kell blood groups. Br J Haematol 1975;29:247-62.

In: Laird-Fryer B, Daniels G and Levitt J, eds.
Blood Group Systems: Kell
Arlington, VA: American Association
of Blood Banks, 1990

4

Defects of McLeod Red Blood Cells and Association With Disease

Philippe Rouger, MD, Biol D

S INCE ITS DISCOVERY BY Coombs, Mourant and Race[1] in 1946, the Kell blood group has increased in complexity. In 1990 this system includes 21 related antigens as described in Chapter 1. The variant called "McLeod," named after the original propositus, was described by Allen et al[2] in 1961. The McLeod phenotype was initially characterized only by severe weakening of Kell blood group antigens. This unusual phenotype is now known to be inherited as an X-linked characteristic with the red blood cells lacking Kx antigen, a product of an X-linked gene.[3,4] Individuals whose red blood cells are of the McLeod phenotype may also develop disease.

McLeod Syndrome: A Hereditary Acanthocytosis

Erythrocytes that are deficient in Kx antigen, produced by the *XK* locus situated on the X chromosome, present a combined deficiency of antigens of the Kell system.[3-5] This phenotype is called McLeod, after the first subject in whom this syndrome was described. McLeod syndrome is also characterized by a morphological abnormality called acanthocytosis (erythrocytes shaped like acanthus leaves) combined with anisocytosis, in-

Philippe Rouger, MD, Biol D, Head, Blood Group Reference Laboratory, Institut National de Transfusion Sanguine, Paris, France

creased osmotic fragility, reticulocytosis, a reduction in serum haptoglobin level and splenomegaly.[6] The individual with the McLeod phenotype usually has well-compensated hemolytic anemia, but on occasion may have severe and sometimes fatal hemolytic anemia. The acanthocytes, which are detectable by light microscopy, have an atypical shape with large irregular projections from the red blood cell surface. It should be emphasized that these abnormalities are not observed in subjects of K_o phenotype whose red blood cells lack Kell antigens but have increased expression of Kx antigen.[7] Thus, it is the deficit in Kx and not the secondary deficit in Kell antigens that is responsible for the abnormality.[4]

Acanthocytes were originally described in a case of beta lipoprotein deficiency and, since then, in a number of classical situations such as hypothyroidism, hepatic diseases with hemolysis and neonatal hepatitis. The pathogenic mechanism inducing acanthocytosis in these diseases is unknown. Data concerning the McLeod phenotype are not much more explicit. In some cases membrane phospholipid has been found to be reduced, but no deficiency in Beta lipoprotein has been observed.

Diagnosis of McLeod Syndrome

During the past few years a clinical entity has been defined that has X-linked inheritance and involves erythropoietic, neurologic and muscular tissues.[8] The association of myopathy in McLeod syndrome cannot be explained. All people with acanthocytic red blood cells and weakness of Kell antigens should be evaluated for McLeod syndrome. Female carriers of the McLeod genetic abnormality have a dual red blood cell population of acanthocytes with the McLeod phenotype and normal discocytes with common Kell type. Recognition of the female carrier, by finding acanthocytes in her peripheral blood, may lead to suspicion of McLeod syndrome in a male infant.[9]

Serological Findings

In most cases, red blood cells of people with McLeod syndrome are: KEL:-1,2,-3,4,-6,7 [K-k+, Kp(a-b+), Js(a-b+)] with weak expression of KEL2, KEL4 and KEL7 antigens. However, Marsh et al[10] reported a family in which two brothers had McLeod syndrome. One was KEL:-1, while the other was the first known KEL:1 subject with McLeod syndrome. The *KEL 1* gene in the latter was expressed weakly and was inherited from the father, in whom it was expressed normally. The brothers had the same clinical and laboratory manifestations of McLeod syndrome but had different *KEL* genes. This finding indicates that the *KEL* gene is unlikely to contribute to the development of McLeod syndrome.

It is of interest that murine monoclonal anti-Kell antibodies, with anti-KEL2 and anti-KEL14 specificity, have little activity for McLeod red blood cells. This marked difference in reactivity of the monoclonal antibodies suggests that the difference in Kell antigens of McLeod red blood cells is both quantitative and qualitative.[9]

Positive identification of the McLeod red blood cell phenotype is made by using an anti-KL serum.[11] The anti-KL contains anti-Kx and anti-KEL20 (anti-Km).[12] Anti-KL is produced by immunized males with both chronic granulomatous disease (CGD) and McLeod syndrome. CGD is inherited as an X-linked condition and has an association with McLeod syndrome. Some males with CGD have red blood cells of the McLeod blood group phenotype.[4,5] Marsh et al[4] demonstrated that in the sera of immunized McLeod CGD patients, the two antibodies could be separated by adsorption-elution procedures. One of these two antibodies, now named anti-KEL20 (anti-Km) could be bound by and eluted from any red blood cells except red blood cells of the McLeod or K_o phenotypes. Thus, this antibody is Kell related.

The other antibody, named anti-Kx, could be bound by and eluted from K_o red blood cells, with which it strongly reacts, but was not as easily adsorbed by red blood cells of common Kell type. Anti-Kx does not agglutinate McLeod red blood cells, but it does weakly agglutinate ordinary Kell red blood cells and strongly agglutinates K_o red blood cells. This suggests that Kell antigens could be built on a Kx substrate, which would not be converted in K_o red blood cells, but would be converted into Kell antigens in common phenotypes. Further evidence of this concept is the fact that Kx antigen expression on red blood cells of individuals heterozygous for *KEL 0*, the gene responsible for the K_o phenotype, is intermediate in strength between that for K_o red blood cells and red blood cells expressing common *KEL* genotype.[7] The relationship of Kx antigen to Kell antigens or the reason why absence of a normal *XK* gene appears to down-regulate expression of the *KEL* genes, is still unknown.

Sullivan et al[13] found an IgG autoantibody with Kx specificity in the blood of a 61-year-old Caucasian male. This antibody did not cause hemolysis of his own or transfused Kx-positive red blood cells. The patient was of common Kell blood group and did not exhibit any clinical or hematological features of McLeod syndrome.

A number of other rare phenotypes exist that are characterized by weakened expression of Kell system antigens (see Chapter 1). Red blood cells of all of these phenotypes differ from McLeod red blood cells by expressing Kx antigen.

Other Anomalies Associated With the McLeod Syndrome

Several observations suggest an association between McLeod syndrome and somewhat ill-defined muscular abnormalities indicative of Duchenne muscular dystrophy (DMD), which progressively develops as the individual grows older.[14] In a similar context, it has been shown that the serum level of creatinine phosphokinase (isoenzyme MM) is abnormally high in McLeod individuals, as is also the case in diverse forms of muscular dystrophy.[15] This enzyme, which allows the synthesis of adenosine triphosphate, is present in high amounts in cardiac and skeletal muscles as well as in the brain. High serum levels of this enzyme usually signify a lesion of one of these tissues. Cardiomyopathy is often a complication. The serum level of carbonic anhydrase III is also increased in McLeod individuals, as it is in patients with muscular dystrophy. Finally, other observations suggest that some persons with McLeod phenotype can have neurological affections, evidenced by choreiform movements and the absence of some tendinal reflexes. These varied biochemical and clinical manifestations are surprising and as yet unexplained in patients in whom the muscular dystrophy locus is not affected.

Swash et al[16] described two heathy men with McLeod syndrome; both men showed raised blood creatinine kinase levels with myopathic electromyographic abnormalities. Biopsies of the quadriceps muscle showed the features of an active myopathy although there was no clinical evidence of muscular abnormality. The combination of the association of membrane abnormalities in red blood cells and a myopathy in both McLeod phenotype and DMD suggested that these syndromes may be due to related genetic abnormalities.

Marked weakness of common red blood cell Kell antigens, together with normal serum beta lipoprotein, a high level of creatinine phosphokinase in the serum, and absence of deep tendon reflexes, is sufficient for the diagnosis of McLeod syndrome in a male with an appropriate hematological picture.

CGD, McLeod Phenotype and Anomalies of the X Chromosome

All known cases of McLeod phenotype were described in males and family studies show that this variant is transmitted through the X chromosome, though the *KEL* locus itself is on an autosome. It has also been demonstrated by Giblett et al[17] that some male children with CGD, a severe sex-linked hereditary illness characterized by a deficiency in bactericidal capacity of polynuclear granulocytes, have the exceptional McLeod phenotype. In fact, these authors reported that the frequency of this phenotype is much higher in individuals with CGD than in the normal population.

The association of these two rare phenomena, even though inconstant, suggests that they could have a common denominator. Since normal polynuclear cells express neither Kx nor Kell antigens, it is clear that these antigens are not implicated in the functional defects of these granulocytes. Recent studies in molecular biology seem to indicate that a deficit of cytochrome b-245 involved in the mechanisms of oxidation reduction and production of oxygen derivatives necessary for the destruction of the microorganisms phagocytized by the granulocytes is implicated in the disease.[18-20,32]

The study of certain rare patients demonstrating an extraordinary association of CGD, McLeod phenotype, retinitis pigmentosa and DMD, indicates the existence of a considerable deletion of the X chromosome and suggests a localization of the genes responsible for these anomalies in the p21 region of the X chromosome.[21] The study of other patients with McLeod syndrome has confirmed the localization of the *XK* gene on Xp21, between the locus for *CGD* and that for *DMD*.[22]

XK, *XG* Genes and X-Inactivation (Lyonization)—Mapping the *McLeod* Gene

It is well-documented that the mothers of children suffering from the sex-linked form of CGD have in their blood a mixture of functional and nonfunctional leukocytes. Mothers of children with McLeod syndrome also have a mixture of erythrocytes, one population with a normal Kell phenotype and the other with McLeod phenotype. This cellular mosaic is easily identifiable by the presence of acanthocytes.[6,23] It has been shown that flow cytometric analysis allows accurate identification of the McLeod carrier state even when the population of

McLeod red blood cells is low. The existence of a dual population of leukocytes and/or erythrocytes in carriers is a result of the phenomenon of lyonization—that is, the random inactivation of the genes of one of the X chromosomes of females.[24]

The study of the expression of blood group Xg[a] indicates a genetic linkage between the XK (Xp21) and XG (Xp22-3 - Xpter) loci, but also indicates that the XG locus remains functional and escapes the lyonization phenomenon. Thus, in a McLeod family studied by Wimer et al,[6] the mother's red blood cells with either normal or McLeod phenotypes were both of Xg(a+) phenotype. Family studies have shown recombination between the XK and XG loci.[25]

In 1985, Francke et al[21] reported a male patient who suffered from CGD associated with cytochrome b-245 deficiency, McLeod syndrome, DMD and retinitis pigmentosa (RP). The cytogenetic analysis seemed to show a very subtle interstitial deletion of part of band 21 of the X chromosome. Since it was impossible to know whether his material was truly deleted or inserted elsewhere in the genome, somatic cell and molecular studies were performed. In somatic cell hybrids, the X chromosome with the interstitial deletion was isolated on a Chinese hamster background. Southern blot analysis with 20 single-copy probes that had been mapped to the X short arm led to the discovery of one probe that is missing from the patient's X chromosome and also from his total DNA. This proves that this patient's X chromosome has a deletion rather than a balanced insertion. The results also provide cytological mapping information for the X-linked phenotypes.

By means of DNA hybridization with a cDNA probe used in a patient suffering from CGD and the McLeod syndrome, Frey et al[26] demonstrated deletion of the X-CGD gene. Thus, the authors suggested that the X-CGD and McLeod loci were physically close in the p21 region of the X chromosome, proximal to the DMD locus (Fig 4-1).

Bertelson et al[22] studied seven males with the McLeod red blood cell phenotype and associated myopathy but without CGD, one male with McLeod phenotype associated with CGD and two males known to possess large deletions of the DMD locus. DNA isolated from each patient was screened for the presence or absence of various cloned sequences located in the Xp21 region of the human X chromosome. Two of the seven males who have only the McLeod phenotype and are cousins exhibit deletions for four Xp21 cloned fragments but are not deleted for any portion of either the CGD or DMD locus. Comparison of the cloned segments absent from these two patients with those absent from the two males with DMD and the

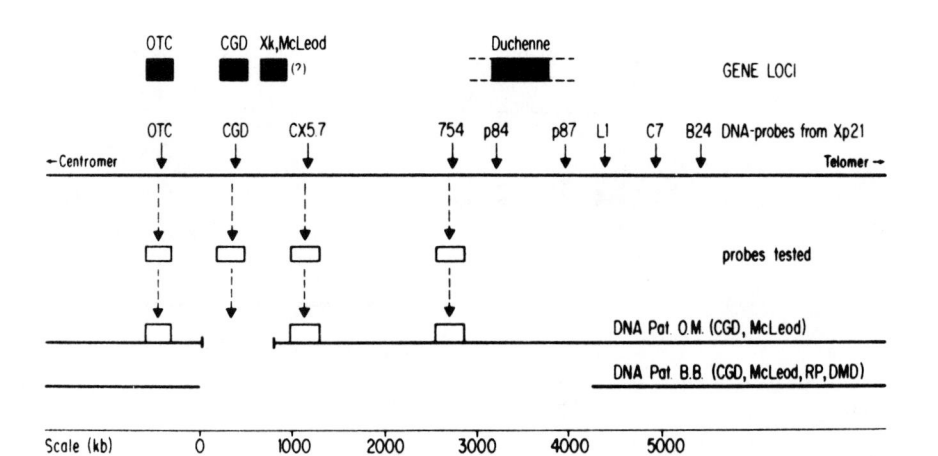

Figure 4-1. Deletion map of Xp21 derived from patients BB and OM described by Frey et al.[26] From top to bottom, black boxes indicate gene loci in Xp21; arrows, DNA probes from Xp21; bottom, DNA of the CGD/McLeod patient (OM) that failed to hybridize with the CGD cDNA probe; and extent of the deletion found in patient BB with RP, CGD, McLeod and DMD. (Reprinted with permission from Frey et al.[26])

patients with CGD/McLeod leads to the submapping of various cloned DNA segments within the Xp21 region. Results of these studies place the locus for the *McLeod* gene within a 500-Kb interval distal from the *CGD* locus toward the *DMD* locus (Fig 4-2).

In 1988, de Saint-Basile et al [27] described the case of a male patient with CGD, RP and McLeod phenotype. The studies of his parents demonstrated the X-linked transmission of these three traits in this family, and a deletion of the entire *X-CGD* gene of the patient's DNA. All but one other DNA markers tested, including those in Xp21, were present. These findings strongly suggest that the *McLeod* locus and at least one X-linked *RP* gene are closely linked to the *X-CGD* locus in the Xp21 region of the human X chromosome.

Biochemical Defects Associated With the McLeod Syndrome

The biochemical origins of the molecular lesion responsible for the abnormal morphology and the increase in osmotic fragility

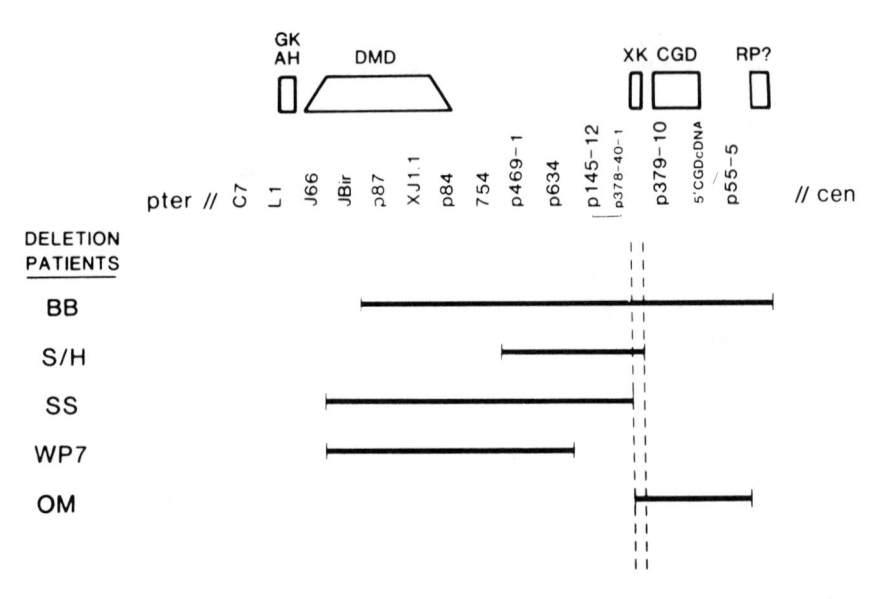

Figure 4-2. Schematic representation of Xp21 disorders and cloned loci. The following disorders are boxed at the top of the figure: Gk, adrenal hypoplasia (AH), DMD, XK, CGD and RP. The cloned DNA segments are aligned below and are spaced equidistant along the chromosome in the figure. The cloned DNA segments include the following DNA segments: C7 (DXS28), LI(DXS68), J66. JBir, p87 (DXS164), XJ1.1 (DXS206), p84 (DXS142), 754 (DXS84, p469-1, p634, p145-12, [DXS141]), P378-40-1, 379-10 (3' CGD cDNA), 5' CGD cDNA, and p55-5 (DXS140). Below the loci are shown the extent of the deletions: patient BB; S/H, cases 1 and 2; SS, case 10; WP7, case 9; and OM, case 8. The location of the McLeod locus is indicated by the dotted vertical lines. GK, AH and DMD were positioned with reference to these cloned DNA segments on the basis of previously published information. (Reprinted with permission from Bertelson et al.[22])

of McLeod red blood cells are still unclear. In spite of these characteristics, active and passive sodium and potassium transport are normal, as are membrane microviscosity and lipid composition.[28] However, a quantitative reduction of total lipids has been observed in some cases.

According to Kuypers et al[29] the acanthocytic McLeod red blood cells appear to have a normal phospholipid composition and distribution. The exchangeability of phosphatidylcholine was found to be markedly enhanced. Unlike control erythrocytes, in which 75% of all of the phosphatidylcholine was exchanged during an 8-hour incubation, the McLeod red blood cells showed a completed exchange of this phospholipid within the same time period. This obviously indicated an enhanced transbilayer mobility of phosphatidylcholine in the membrane of McLeod red blood cells.

In normal red blood cells, dimyriotoyl phosphatidylserine (DMPS) is transported across the membrane by an enzymatic process and accumulates in the inner leaflet of the membrane bilayer, causing discocyte-to-stomatocyte shape change. Redman et al[30] demonstrated that scanning electron microscopy of McLeod red blood cells shows a mixture composed of 15% discocytes, 51% red blood cells with irregular surfaces and 34% acanthocytes. On incubation with various concentrations of DMPS, McLeod red blood cells transported DMPS across the membrane, which caused irregularly shaped and acanthocytic McLeod red blood cells to attain normal discocyte shape and later to become stomatocytes. Chlorpromazine had a similar effect on the shape of McLeod red blood cells. This suggests that in McLeod red blood cells, acanthocytosis is due to a lack of lipid in the inner leaflet of the membrane bilayer but that the imbalance is not caused by defective transport of phosphatidylserine across the membrane. It is not known whether the absence of Kx protein is responsible for these abnormal findings.

Recently it has been shown that a 37-kDa glycoprotein recognized by anti-Kx antibody was missing from the surface of McLeod red blood cells.[31] The 37-kDa protein might represent the direct product of the XK gene. Kell protein (93 kDa) is present on McLeod red blood cells but in reduced amounts. The absence of Kx antigen was demonstrated by immunoprecipitation with human alloimmune anti-Kx, followed by isolation of immune complexes from detergent-solubilized red blood cell membranes with protein A Sepharose. Eluted immune complexes were then analyzed by sodium dodecylsulfate polyacrylamide gel electrophoresis (SDS-PAGE) under reducing conditions.

The near-neighbor relationship of McLeod phenotype and common Kell red blood cell membrane proteins was also studied by crosslinking intrinsic sulphydryl groups or by crosslinking amino groups. Results were analyzed by diagonal mapping in two dimensional gels. No abnormalities of membrane protein interrelationship were detected in McLeod red blood cells.

The relation between Kell and Kx proteins is not yet elucidated, though the two molecules would seem to exist in the membrane as a heterodimeric complex maintained by a disulfide bond. It remains to be understood how Kx can be normally expressed in the absence of Kell protein (K_o individuals) and why Kx seems essential for the correct expression of Kell antigens (McLeod individuals). In fact, the most common form of CGD is an abnormality of the membrane-associated heavy chain (91 kDa) of cytochrome b-588.[32]

Conclusion

The study of the McLeod variant is fascinating. McLeod red blood cells have abnormal morphology, biochemical defects and decreased in vivo survival. Association of the McLeod phenotype with neurological disorders and CGD is well-documented, but more is to be learned about the biochemistry and genetics. Further research is needed to determine the function of the Kx antigen in the red blood cell membrane and the relationship of the *XK* gene and clinical disease.

References

1. Coombs RRA, Mourant AE, Race RR. In vivo isosensitization of red cells in babies with haemolytic disease.Lancet 1946;1:264-6.
2. Allen FH Jr, Krabbe SMR, Corcoran PA. A new phenotype (McLeod) in the Kell blood group system. Vox Sang 1961; 6:555-60.
3. Marsh WL, Taswell HF, Øyen R, et al. Kx antigen of the Kell system and its relationship to chronic granulomatous disease: Evidence that the Kx gene is X-linked (abstract). Transfusion 1975;15:527.
4. Marsh WL, Øyen R, Nichols ME, Allen FH Jr. Chronic granulomatous disease and the Kell blood groups. Br J Haematol 1975;29:247-62.
5. Marsh WL, Øyen R, Nichols ME. Kx antigen. The McLeod phenotype and chronic granulomatous disease: Further studies. Vox Sang 1976;31:356-62.
6. Wimer BM, Marsh WL, Taswell HF, Galey WR. Hematological changes associated with the McLeod phenotype of the Kell blood group system. Br J Haematol 1977;36:219-24.
7. Marsh WL. The Kell blood groups and their relationship to chronic granulomatous disease. In: Steane EA, ed. Cellular antigens and disease. Washington, DC: American Association of Blood Banks 1977:52-66.
8. Marsh WL. Deleted antigens of the Rhesus and Kell blood groups: Association with cell membrane defects. In: Blood group antigens and disease. Arlington, VA: American Association of Blood Banks, 1983:165-85.

9. Marsh WL. Cold agglutinins to Kell: 35 years as a serologist. In: Moore SB, ed. Progress in immunohematology. Arlington, VA: American Association of Blood Banks, 1988: 93-117.

10. Marsh WL, Schnipper EF, Johnson CL, et al. An individual with McLeod syndrome and the Kell blood group antigen K(K1). Transfusion 1983;23:336-8.

11. Hart Van der M, Szaloky A, Van Loghem JM. A new antibody associated with the Kell blood group system. Vox Sang 1968;15:456-8.

12. Marsh WL. Kell system notation. Vox Sang 1979;36:375-6.

13. Sullivan CM, Kline WE, Rabin BI, et al. The first example of auto-anti-Kx. Transfusion 1987;27:322-4.

14. Marsh WL. Molecular defects associated with the McLeod blood group phenotype. In: Salmon C, ed. Blood groups and other red cell surface markers in health and disease. New York: Masson, 1982:17-28.

15. Marsh WL, Marsh NJ, Moore A, et al. Elevated serum creatine phosphokinase in subjects with McLeod syndrome. Vox Sang 1981;40:403-11.

16. Swash M, Shwartz MS, Carter ND, et al. Benign X-linked myopathy with acanthocytes (McLeod syndrome). Its relations to X-linked muscular dystrophy. Brain 1983:106: 717-33.

17. Giblett ER, Klebanoff SJ, Pincus SH, et al. Kell phenotypes in chronic granulomatous disease: A potential transfusion hazard. Lancet 1971;1:1235-6.

18. Segal AW, Cross AR, Garcia RC, et al. Absence of cytochrome b-245 in chronic granulomatous disease. N Engl J Med 1983;308:245-51.

19. Ohno Y, Buescher ES, Roberts R, et al. Reevaluation of cytochrome band flavine adenine dinucleotide in neutrophils from patients with chronic granulomatous disease and description of a family with probable autosomal recessive inheritance of cytochrome b deficiency. Blood 1983; 67:1132-8.

20. Bohler MC, Seger R, Moug R, et al. A study of 25 patients with chronic granulomatous disease: new classification by correlating respiratory burst, cytochrome b and favoprotein. J Clin Immunol 1986;6:136-45.

21. Francke U, Ochs HD, Martinville BD, et al. Minor Xp21 chromosome deletion in a male associated with expression of Duchenne muscular dystrophy, chronic granulomatous disease, retinitis pigmentosa and McLeod syndrome. Am J Hum Genet 1985;37:250-67.

22. Bertelson CJ, Pogo AD, Chandhuri A, et al. Localization of the McLeod Locus (XK) within XP21 by deletion analysis. Am J Hum Genet 1988;42:703-11.
23. Symmans WA, Shepherd CS, Marsh WL, et al. Hereditary acanthocytosis associated with the McLeod phenotype of the Kell blood group system. Br J Haematol 1979;42:575-83.
24. Lyon M. Genetic factors of the X-chromosome. Lancet 1961;2:434-7.
25. Tippett P. Chromosomal mapping of the blood group genes. Semin Haematol 1981;18:4-12.
26. Frey D, Machler M, Seger R, et al. Gene deletion in a patient with chronic granulomatous disease and McLeod syndrome: Fine mapping of the Xk gene locus. Blood 1988;71:252-5.
27. de Saint-Basile G, Bohler MC, Fisher A, et al. Xp21 DNA microdeletion in a patient with chronic granulomatous disease, retinis pigmentosa, and McLeod phenotype. Hum Genet 1988;80:85-9.
28. Galey WR, Evan AP, Van Nice PS, et al. Morphology and physiology of the McLeod erythrocyte. I. Scanning electron microscopy and electrolyte and water transport properties. Vox Sang 1978;34:152-61.
29. Kuypers FA, Sibenius Trip M, Roelofson B, et al. The phospholipid organization in the membrane of McLeod and Leach phenotype erythrocytes FEBS Lett 1985;184:20-6.
30. Redman CM, Huima T, Robbins E, et al. Effects of phosphatidylserine on the shape of McLeod red cell acanthocytosis. Blood 1989;74:1826-35.
31. Redman CM, Marsh WL, Scarborough A, et al. Biochemical studies an McLeod phenotype red cells and isolation of Kx antigen. Br J Haematol 1988;68:131-6.
32. Gallin JI, Malech HL. Update on chronic granulomatous diseases of childhood. Immunotherapy and potential for gene therapy. JAMA 1990;263:1533-7.

Index

(Italicized page numbers indicate tables or figures.)